MW01118307

Finance's Wrong Turns

Richard O. Michaud

Finance's Wrong Turns

A New Foundation for Financial Markets, Asset Management, and Social Science

Richard O. Michaud
New Frontier Advisors
Boston, MA, USA

ISBN 978-3-031-21862-0   ISBN 978-3-031-21863-7   (eBook)
https://doi.org/10.1007/978-3-031-21863-7

This Palgrave Macmillan imprint is published by the registered company Springer Nature Switzerland AG
The registered company address is: Gewerbestrasse 11, 6330 Cham, Switzerland

To the cherished memory of my mother and father:
Helena Talbot (Pelletier) Michaud
Omer Alexander Michaud

Preface

There is a foundational crisis in financial theory and professional investment practice. There is little if any credible evidence that active investment strategies and traditional institutional quantitative technologies can provide superior risk-adjusted, cost-adjusted return over investment relevant horizons. Behavioral rationales based on presumed existence of investor decision biases are misdirected and add little to improved practice. Investors increasingly adopt minimal cost no-information index or rule-based factor fund investments. Why are investors ignoring professional asset management? What risks exist for algorithmic or self-advised investors for meeting long-term objectives? Can professional asset management be justified?

Economic Theory Status

Economic and financial theory has been in error for more than sixty years and is the fundamental cause of the persistent ineffectiveness of professional asset management. Game theory axioms that claimed to define rational economic thought are now understood to be inconsistent with persistent patterns of economic behavior. Social science is not physics. Human cognition in financial markets and economic activity is the consequence of a collective consciousness resulting from interactions among people and their environment. The foundations of rational investor behavior in financial markets and economics in the work of the early masters of social science such as Durkheim, Knight, Keynes, and Markowitz in an evolving sociological framework were ignored. The enormous institutional quantitative investment management industry that arose in the early 1970s, derivative of flawed behavioral theory, unsurprisingly often failed to provide persistent cost-adjusted value in practice. Essentially finance and social science needed to back up before being set on a more productive and useful path.

Social Science and the Workbench

Contemporary sociological and economic theory, agent-based modeling, and an appreciation of the social context for preference theory can provide a rational and intuitive framework for understanding financial markets and economic behavior. The author narrates his long-term experience in the use and limitations of traditional tools of quantitative asset management as an institutional asset manager and quantitative analyst and strategist on Wall Street. Monte Carlo simulation methods, modern statistical tools, and U.S. patented innovations are introduced to redefine portfolio optimality and procedures for enhanced professional asset management. A new sociological context for exchange and focus on collective rational behavior leads to a novel understanding of modern equity markets as a financial intermediary for time-shift investing, uniquely appropriate for meeting investors' long-term investment objectives.

Overview

The text consists of eight chapters that address the limitations and indicated resolutions for more useful financial theory and more reliable asset management technology. In the process, we trace the major historical developments of theory and institutional asset management practice and their limitations over the course of the twentieth century to the present.

Analytical Requirements

The presentation level requires familiarity with modern financial concepts at an undergraduate finance level, investment professional, or CFA Level I. There are no mathematical derivations or theorems. The discussion remains at an intuitive level with exceptions largely banished to footnotes or appendices.

Boston, USA   Richard O. Michaud

Acknowledgments

I owe my greatest debt to my long-term collaborators and business partners: Robert Michaud (son) and Dr. David Esch. I have benefited from many discussions with Jack Treynor, J. Peter Williamson, Harry Markowitz, Charles D'Ambrosio, Roger Murray, John O'Brien, Gary Bergstrom, Keith Smith, C. Michael Carty, John Guerard, David Tierney, Stephanie Fields, and supporters of my work at the Q-Group, JOIM, CFA Society Boston and New York and Boston professional communities. My mathematical maturity was most influenced by Robin Esch and Flavio Reis. I have greatly benefited from the support of my work associates Neha Sharma, Nick Lam, Joy Zheng, and Cindy Miller. I am deeply grateful to my Boston doctors Allan Pineda, Deborah Jacobs, John Levinson, Martin Ostro, and members of the cardiac team at Mass General. COVID-19 has been a trial while writing this text and I could not have survived emotionally and productively without the support of my daughter Christine Louise Michaud, MD, my wife Brigida Maria Silva Michaud, and the encouragement of the Editor Tula Weis at Palgrave Macmillan.

Contents

About the Author

Dr. Richard O. Michaud is President, Founder, and Chief Executive Officer of New Frontier Advisors. He earned a PhD in Mathematics and Statistics from Boston University and has taught investment management at Columbia University. His research and consulting have focused on asset allocation, investment strategies, global investment management, optimization, stock valuation, and trading costs. He is the author of *Efficient Asset Management* (Harvard 1998, 2nd ed. Oxford 2008 with Robert Michaud), *Investment Styles, Market Anomalies, and Global Stock Selection* (CFA Research Monograph 1999), and over sixty published journal articles, manuscripts, and white papers available at SSRN.com and Researchgate.com and on the www.newfrontieradvisors.com website. He is co-holder of four U.S. patents in portfolio optimization and asset management, a Graham and Dodd Scroll winner for his work on optimization, a former editorial board member of the *Financial Analysts Journal*, associate editor of the *Journal of Investment Management*, and former director of the "Q" Group. Dr. Michaud's research was recently profiled in *WatersTechnology* 2019: "Rebel Math." Notable press articles also include *Institutional Investor 2010*: *Modern Portfolio Theory's Evolutionary Road*, and *Pensions & Investments 2003* "*Markowitz says Michaud has built a better mousetrap.*"

List of Figures

1

The Birth of Modern Finance

The stock market fascinates many people. Stories of fabulous wealth and horrible scams and losses are part of the lore of the "market." Families that have acquired unbelievable wealth seem often to be associated with clever investments. Successful investors are often treated like celebrities in tabloids who attract others looking to get in on the "action." In contrast, many view the stock market as nothing more than a rigged casino roulette game where the average player loses to the house. There are no flashing lights and sirens announcing winners as in a casino, but newspapers find interest in get rich stories, whether based on luck, legacy, or innovation. Is the market a safe place for thoughtful participants? Is it all a marketing scam? Or is there a scientific basis and a set of principles and procedures that would likely reward diligence? Is it possible that proper investing can be a route to saving for a comfortable retirement? Unlike mathematical sciences reputed to be a young person's game, investment management as a discipline tends to reward years of stock market experience.

Rational Investing

Modern finance was born with the publication of Markowitz (1952a). Prior to Markowitz, finance was security valuation theory with Graham and Dodd (1934) and J. B. Williams (1938). Markowitz was a brainy and mathematically facile PhD student in his early twenties at the University of Chicago

© The Author(s), under exclusive license to Springer Nature
Switzerland AG 2023
R. O. Michaud, *Finance's Wrong Turns*,
https://doi.org/10.1007/978-3-031-21863-7_1

looking for a thesis in economics. Someone suggested that he investigates the stock market. Sitting in the University of Chicago's Business School library, he began by asking himself the question: How do mutual fund managers think?

Before we begin our journey tracing modern finance and social science in the twentieth century and beyond, it is useful to consider for a moment: What kind of question is Markowitz asking himself? He was a PhD student in the economics department and steeped in economic theory and Bayesian statistics. While the stock market is about financial transactions, is the social behavior of mutual fund managers' economics? Since the question is about how professional investors behave in a financial market, is it psychology? Since the question concerns the behavior of a group of presumably informed agents in a market, is it sociology? The question seems hardly a natural one for a mathematically gifted student in economics. Or is it possible that, while the question was not about financial economics at the time, perhaps it was what in part it should or would become? We shall wish to revisit the Markowitz question and this transcendent moment in the history of social science in the twentieth century further in our text.

Birth of Modern Finance

Markowitz focused on defining the characteristics of institutional mutual fund management as a reflection of informed stock market behavior. There was no issue of rationality. These were successful business professionals performing a widely successful service.

Stock mutual funds are diversified portfolios chosen for enhanced return relative to an index or level of investment risk. From a mathematical perspective, the mutual funds are budget constrained (BC only) or sum-to-one[1] allocations and avoid short-selling (long-only). Overall portfolio risk varies roughly with the volatility or perceived riskiness of the stocks included in the fund.

In what Markowitz calls his epiphany while sitting in the Chicago Business Library—the moment of birth of modern finance—he understood that parametric quadratic programming (QP), a generalization of linear programming methods that includes the variance of the assets, was consistent with mutual fund management behavior. Maximizing expected return, relative to

---

[1] "Sum to one" refers to all asset weights adding to one. The weight is determined by dividing the dollar amount invested in a particular asset class, divided by the total dollar size of the portfolio.

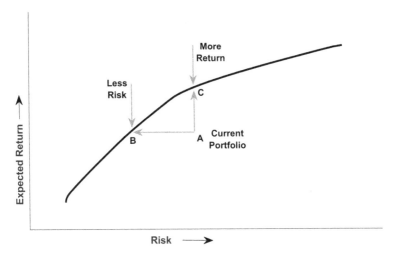

Fig. 1.1 Markowitz mean-variance efficient frontier

the variance of return of the portfolio, subject to sum-to-one and no short-selling constraints, was a computer algorithm as a mathematical model and entirely consistent with institutional mutual fund investment behavior as understood at that time. It was the moment when Markowitz invented the iconic Markowitz mean-variance (MV) efficient frontier.[2]

The Markowitz MV Efficient Frontier

Figure 1.1 displays the Markowitz MV efficient frontier. The horizontal axis represents portfolio risk (standard deviation of portfolio return) and the vertical axis expected or estimated portfolio return. The MV efficient frontier curve represents all optimal portfolios with maximum expected return for a given level of portfolio risk (or conversely minimum risk for a given level of return) subject to a sum-to-one and non-negative allocation constraint.

For many reading this narrative in the first quarter of the twenty-first century, the invention of the Markowitz MV efficient frontier as a model of informed investment behavior may seem self-evident. But the Markowitz frontier is much more than a simple theoretical framework describing institutional mutual fund manager behavior. Markowitz provided investors with a mathematical framework for duplicating the activity of institutional asset managers, in the process creating the quantitative asset management industry.

---

[2] Michaud (2011).

Markowitz also identified the portfolio as the relevant focus of modern finance and risk management as the essential objective of modern asset management. Moreover, the MV efficient frontier can theoretically represent a universal framework for portfolio choice. For example, fixed income, real estate, value, and low volatility securities or strategies may be assumed to populate the lower end of the frontier, growth stocks and emerging market strategies at the higher end, and large cap domestic and international funds in the middle of the frontier. Not a bad day for a brainy twenty something year old economics student sitting in Chicago's Business Library.

A Different Narrative

Our presentation of Markowitz (1952a) reflects a very different narrative from that typically described in standard finance textbooks and academic and professional presentations. Markowitz efficiency is usually taught as requiring significant assumptions for use in theory and applications, but none of the standard conditionals are in fact required. Markowitz MV portfolio theory is no more but no less than a mathematical model of institutional investment behavior of informed agents in a large capital market. It requires no assumption of a specific utility function, normal or other return distribution, or specific risk model. It is not only useful for historical data as sometimes claimed. It is simply a framework that describes how rational informed investors behave when managing a client's money at large financial institutions.

It is worth a moment of reflection to think about this momentous event in social science. In many cases, mathematical models of human behavior have been applications of game theory rationality axioms in economics, psychology, finance, and sociology. While not understood at the time, Markowitz's invention could have been viewed as a contribution to the budding fields of mathematical psychology and sociology. In any event, the Markowitz epiphany was unarguably a protean moment for modern finance as we understand today and, as we will argue, one of the most foundational events in all of twentieth-century social science.

There is another interesting aspect of this moment in finance worth noting. There is a long history of amateur investors attempting to use mathematical formulas to beat the market. The Markowitz epiphany can be viewed as a prime example of a mathematically gifted and computer savvy investor. It would not be the last time it would happen. Professional asset management would never be the same.

The Critical Line Algorithm

The Markowitz (1952a) proposal of a quadratic programming framework to replicate institutional mutual fund management had several limitations in practice. From a contemporary perspective, computational methods at the time were primitive and practical applications were therefore limited. But the Markowitz frontier also had a subtle but important conceptual limitation. While there were computational algorithms that could solve a quadratic programming problem for a specific point on the Markowitz curve, the Markowitz efficient frontier conceptually represented the locus of all possible sign and BC only efficiently diversified portfolios.[3]

From a theoretical framework, the Markowitz MV efficient frontier is definable in terms of parametric quadratic programming. In a standard formulation, the objective function is defined as maximizing mean portfolio return μ_p minus the risk aversion parameter, λ, times the portfolio variance σ_p^2. The goal is to find all portfolios $(\mu_p \sigma_p)$ that maximize

$$\text{Max } \phi = \mu_p - \lambda \sigma_p^2 \tag{1.1}$$

for parameter values of λ from 0 to infinity. The solutions of (1.1) trace the MV efficient frontier in Fig. 1.1 from the maximum expected return portfolio at the top of the curve to the minimum variance or standard deviation portfolio at the bottom of the curve. Prior to Markowitz, no computationally efficient procedure existed for solving the problem of computing all the efficient portfolios for all possible levels of investor risk aversion in one computation.

Markowitz (1955, 1959 Appendix B) proposed the Critical Line Algorithm (CLA) variation of the quadratic programming algorithm for computing the entire set of MV efficient portfolios. His new algorithm provides an efficient and convenient computational method for finding all the optimized portfolios. The CLA was a major achievement and won the Von Neumann prize in computer science two years prior to Markowitz's being awarded the Nobel Prize in economics in 1990. In many cases, the CLA remains today the recommended method of choice for computing the sign and MV efficient frontier.

---

[3] Beale (1955, 1959) and Wolfe (1959) provide alternative quadratic programming procedures during this period.

Scientific Investment Management

While Markowitz (1952a) was a major theoretical achievement, it was not much more than a sketch for a scientific framework for practical institutional asset management. There were many important issues that needed to be addressed well beyond the scope of the 1952a paper.[4]

Markowitz (1959) presents a range of issues and innovations that follow from the fundamental concept of the MV efficient frontier. The monograph can be seen as a manifesto for scientific asset management. It includes major advances in financial theory and a well-marked trail for a quantitative approach to asset management.

The monograph is roughly one-third discussion of stock risk-return estimation, one-third computation of MV efficient portfolios, and one-third expected utility theory and application. The first section includes the notion of a linear model of expected return relative to an index (Markowitz 1959, pp. 97–101) anticipating the influential Sharpe (1963) market line model; the Law of the Average Covariance (Markowitz 1959, Ch. 5) that leads to the market index CAPM framework; and the importance of the geometric mean (Markowitz 1959, Ch. 6) for selecting "most optimal" long-term investment portfolios on the MV efficient frontier. The second section describes the geometric character of efficient sets and derivation of efficient portfolios while noting the semi-variance as an alternative risk measure. The final section addresses advanced issues of rational decision making under uncertainty including objections to the von Neumann-Morgenstern (1944) game theory axioms, the Savage (1954) contributions for personal probability axioms, the dynamic programming framework for rationalizing optimal long-term single-period MV optimization, and discussion of expected utility applications to portfolio selection with the critical line algorithm in the Appendix.

While Markowitz is undisputedly the father of modern portfolio theory, it may be surprising to many readers to know that the investment community largely ignored his framework as a practical approach to scientific asset management. Many of the innovations in investment technology in the twentieth century mostly ignored Markowitz's vision for quantitative asset management. We will address many of these issues in the following chapters of the text.

---

[4] Markowitz (1952b) addresses expected utility issues and rational decision making.

Well-Defined Investment Programs—A Technical Note

We will use the term "well-defined investment program" to refer to a MV optimization of desirable investments appropriate for Markowitz MV optimization. This phrase is generally considered to include market priced securities such as common stocks, bonds, index funds, exchange-traded funds, and variations on similar themes. The objective of Markowitz optimization is to define a successful investment strategy. In this regard, it is often considered inappropriate to include non-transparent, non-market priced securities or contingent claims. In addition, an MV optimization can be badly defined. Consider including negative return assets for defining a long-only investment strategy.[5] More generally, an MV optimization may be most useful when the optimization universe consists of relatively similar magnitude estimated risks and returns.

References

Beale, E.M.L. 1955. On Minimizing a Convex Function Subject to Linear Inequalities. *Journal of the Royal Statistical Society (B)* 17: 173–184.

Beale, E.M.L. 1959. On Quadratic Programming. *Naval Research Logistics Quarterly* 6 (3): 227–243.

Graham, B., and D. Dodd. 1934. *Security Analysis: Principles and Techniques.* New York: McGraw-Hill.

Markowitz, H. 1952a. Portfolio Selection. *Journal of Finance* 7 (1): 77–91.

Markowitz, H. 1952b. Utility of Wealth. *Journal of Political Economy* 60 (2): 151–158.

Markowitz, H. 1955. The Optimization of a Quadratic Function Subject to Linear Constraints. *Naval Research Logistics Quarterly* 3: 111–133.

Markowitz, H. 1959. *Portfolio Selection: Efficient Diversification of Investments,* 2nd ed. New York and Cambridge MA: Wiley and Basil Blackwell.

Michaud, R. 1993. Are Long-Short Equity Strategies Superior? *Financial Analyst Journal* 49 (6): 44–49.

Michaud, R. 2011. Dr. Harry M. Markowitz Interview with Dr. Richard O. Michaud. JOIM Conference Series San Diego, March 6. *Journal of Investment Management* 9 (4): 1–9. Available at SSRN: https://ssrn.com/abstract=2402240 or https://doi.org/10.2139/ssrn.2402240.

Savage, L.J. 1954. *Foundations of Statistics.* NY: Wiley.

---

[5] Negative return assets can be considered appropriate in a well-defined investment program in the context of a long-short investment strategy. See Michaud (1993).

Sharpe, W. 1963. A Simplified Model for Portfolio Analysis. *Management Science* 9: 277–293.

Von Neumann, J., and O. Morgenstern. 1944. *Theory of Games and Economic Behavior*. Princeton: Princeton University Press.

Williams, J.B. 1938. *Theory of Investment Value*. Cambridge, MA: Harvard University Press.

Wolfe, P. 1959. The Simplex Algorithm for Quadratic Programming. *Econometrica* 27 (3): 382–398.

2

Capital Market Theory and Efficient Markets

Markowitz (1959) represented an explosion of ideas and a well-founded set of proposals for a theory of finance and a scientific approach to asset management. But finance took a sharp turn from the path that Markowitz had outlined. There were two dominant new ideas—the Capital Asset Pricing Model (CAPM) and efficient markets. Both emerged post-1960 and would characterize finance theory and supply the tools for investment management in the remainder of the twentieth century and beyond.

Capital Asset Pricing Model (CAPM)

The Capital Asset Pricing Model (CAPM) of Sharpe (1964), Lintner (1965), Treynor (1963), and Mossin (1966) uses, as a starting point, the notion of the Markowitz (1952, 1959) mean-variance (MV) efficient frontier. CAPM is an elegant and attractive theoretical framework for modern finance that motivated much of the development of twentieth-century financial technology.

The theorems associated with CAPM are based on neoclassical economics expected utility theory. Neoclassical economics has a long and revered history. Economic value has been historically based on mathematical models for utility maximization.[1] Utility functions have a long history in probability theory and the notion of rational decision-making under uncertainty. Such

---

[1] Walras (1874) and Menger (1892).

concepts have been a productive theory of fundamental economic and financial concepts.

The CAPM starting point is the concept of the MV efficient frontier and generally considered the successor to Markowitz theory. The main results follow from basic rationality principles and simple MV portfolio optimization assumptions.

In his introduction, Sharpe (1964) clearly states his objective: "At present there is no theory describing the manner in which the price of risk results from the basic influences of investor preferences …." He outlines his proposal as: "Markowitz, following von Neumann and Morgenstern (VM), developed an analysis based on the expected utility maxim and proposed a general solution for the portfolio selection problem." CAPM is known as neoclassical economics expected utility preference theory because of its foundational assumptions on VM game theory rationality for investor choice behavior.

CAPM Utility Assumptions

Sharpe (1964) assumes that each investor's expected utility U of portfolio return r, E(U(r)), follows VM game theory rationality axioms for "correct" decision making under uncertainty. To develop CAPM theory, Sharpe makes two crucial simplifying assumptions concerning investor expected utility. Expected utility of BC only MV optimized portfolio return can be approximated as:

1. A function of the mean and variance of return and
2. A quadratic utility function of the mean and variance.

More specifically:

$$E(U(r)) \approx E\left(U\left(\mu_p, \sigma_p^2\right)\right) \approx \mu_p - \lambda\sigma_p^2 \qquad (2.1)$$

where λ is a parameter denoting the investor's level of risk aversion.

Note that the approximation of the expected utility of return function (2.1) is exactly the Markowitz MV efficient frontier objective function (1.1). Consequently, maximization of expected utility in the CAPM is exactly BC only Markowitz MV optimization. For analytical convenience in CAPM theory, the sign constraint is not included in the formulation of expected utility. This crucial difference will turn out to be highly significant later in our narrative. In the usual formulation, CAPM also assumes a riskless rate asset r_0.

CAPM Formulas

Compute the BC only MV efficient frontier and draw a straight line from r_0, the return of the riskless asset, to the tangent optimal portfolio M with expected return $\mu_{M\leftarrow}$ on the BC only MV efficient frontier illustrated in Fig. 2.1. Assuming unconstrained borrowing and lending, the line extending from r_0 to the tangent portfolio M on the MV efficient frontier and beyond is called the Capital Market Line (CML). The CML represents the expected return μ_p of BC only MV efficient portfolios p. In the construction, CML portfolios equal or dominate the MV efficiency of Markowitz MV efficient frontier portfolios at all levels of investment risk. Sharpe further assumes that investors have homogeneous expectations and that the market is in equilibrium so that the optimal portfolio M with return μ_M is the clearing or "market" portfolio in (2.2) and Fig. 2.1.

$$E(\mu_P) = r_0 + \sigma_p(\mu_M - r_0)/\sigma_M \qquad (2.2)$$

for any portfolio p on the CM

To derive the relationship of individual security risk with expected return, Sharpe defines a continuous function $f(x) = x^*a + (1 - x)^*g$ where a is any individual asset, g is a MV efficient portfolio, and b is the portfolio at $x = -1$ where b is a portfolio that does not include asset a and $f(0)$ is tangent to the market line as illustrated in Fig. 2.2. With simple calculus and analysis,

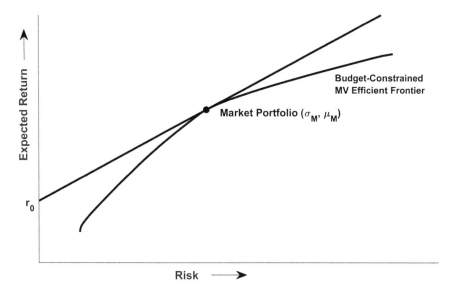

Fig. 2.1 Capital market line $\mu_P = \sigma_P(\mu_M - r_0)/\sigma_M$

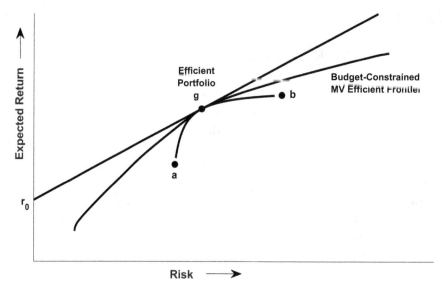

Fig. 2.2 Sharpe (1964) security market line proof $E(r_i) = r_0 + \beta_i(\mu_M - r_0)$

Sharpe is able to derive the famous Security Market Line (SML) formula. The formula (2.3) graphed in Fig. 2.2 implies that the expected return of any security i can be uniquely described as a function of the "beta" of the security, return on the market portfolio, and the risk-free rate:

$$E(r_i) = r_0 + \beta_i(\mu_M - r_0) \tag{2.3}$$

β_i is the measure of undiversifiable risk of the security, often approximated as $\beta_i = \rho_i\sigma_i/\sigma_M$ where ρ_i is the correlation of security i with the market portfolio.

CAPM Status

The CAPM was a major theoretical achievement that continues to dominate financial theory and institutional investment practice. It is a simple theoretically elegant framework taught in virtually all reputable academic programs in modern finance. It has also been a boon to asset management in practice. The astonishing result of the theory is that the expected return of any financial security can be computed simply from an estimate of the security's beta.

Practical Implications

A straightforward interpretation of a security's beta is that it is the regression coefficient of a linear regression of time-series returns, relative to market portfolio or index returns, and the riskless rate. An estimate of expected return for a security or portfolio allows estimation of "alpha" or "active" return as the difference between average return and beta-adjusted return. All these concepts are of great utility to practitioners and account for a dramatic rise in institutional quantitative asset management.

The CAPM assumptions of homogenous expectations and clearing markets in equilibrium, not part of Markowitz theory, are generally rationalized as necessary conventions for developing a theoretical framework. More significantly, CAPM is based on VM game theory axioms. VM game theory is very fashionable among social science theoreticians. Beginning with Samuelson (1948), VM quickly gained academic authority among theoretical and working economists as the framework of choice for understanding rational economic behavior. Game theory axioms are sharply different from the three Markowitz behavioral axioms. VM axioms may seem a far more sophisticated framework for defining a scientific theory than the direct even homespun character of the Markowitz axioms associated with the behavior of mutual fund managers.

Markowitz theory and CAPM theory have important similarities. Each is based on portfolio choice relative to a quadratic utility function of the mean and variance of return with the parameter representing investor risk aversion. But there is one crucial difference. CAPM theory ignores the long-only constraint in Markowitz theory for analytical convenience. The sign constraint, a necessary condition for consistency with institutional asset management behavior, requires linear and quadratic programming methods for computation. In contrast, calculus is all that is necessary for computing CAPM theorems.

At the time, few seemed to notice or be concerned that something fundamentally different from Markowitz theory had been assumed. But it was, as we will argue, the moment of finance's first theoretical wrong turn in the twentieth century. Markowitz theory and the CAPM are fundamentally different in assumptions and implications. As we will discuss in Chapter 3, the institutional quantitative investment revolution that Markowitz might have reasonably thought he enabled with the invention of the CLA in Markowitz (1956, 1959) turned out to be no match for the theoretical power and practical intuitive appeal of the CAPM concepts that were to be developed for investment practice.

Efficient Markets Hypothesis

A closely associated academic theory to CAPM is the Efficient Market Hypothesis (EMH). The EMH proposes that all available information about a security is reflected in its current price. Any attempt to use current information to anticipate future price changes is unlikely to be reliably successful. The EMH, most associated with Samuelson (1965) and Fama (1970), has its roots in the random walk hypothesis from Bachelier (1900), Roberts (1959), and many others. While the price series of a stock or index may seem relatable to various events in the economy or social context over time, the price change of the series often appears remarkably like a pure random process.

The basic principle of efficient markets price informational efficiency is a useful first approximation in a manager's search for factors that may be affecting security price. An important reason for the dominance of the EMH in academia is its consistency with CAPM theory. As CAPM explains, in equilibrium, stock beta is all that is necessary to estimate expected return. But the most convincing evidence for the EMH has been that it is hard to beat in careful studies of manager performance in practice. There is little convincing empirical evidence of manager outperformance over investor relevant horizons on a risk-adjusted and cost-adjusted basis. The Scotch verdict is that capital markets are EMH consistent and CAPM provides all that is relevant about financial markets.

But from basic financial intuition and investment experience, at the extreme, the EMH seems clearly wrong. The Internet bubble, the 2008 to 2009 market meltdown, the one-day collapse of the market on October 19, 1987, and many other examples of extreme market volatility indicate that EMH consistency is not very believable either. Is there a possible resolution of this conundrum?

An Academy-Workbench Truce

A kind of EMH truce exists between a nothing-works efficient market academic mantra and professional asset management. As Grossman and Stiglitz (1986) show: "Informationally Efficient Markets are Impossible." The market would collapse if there were no information in the market. A non-degenerate market equilibrium can only arise when there are sufficient profit opportunities to compensate for costs. In addition, Campbell et al. (1997) show that, even if abnormal returns necessary to compensate for information costs exist, the profits may not be abnormal when costs are accounted for.

The EMH is a favorite academic theory that provides a handy explanation why it is not very necessary to worry about claims of consistent risk-adjusted superior investment performance. On the other hand, from the perspective of the workbench, the EMH is a useful rule of thumb for understanding financial paradoxes in everyday practice. Every serious investment professional in finance uses EMH thinking. It provides a benchmark to determine why something is priced as it is to search for an explanation when something doesn't seem to make sense. But the conundrum of few examples of successful investment practice, the bulk of the argument of proponents of EMH, can be convincingly rationalized, as we will do in following chapters, in terms of failed financial theory and pervasive, and provably ineffective, twentieth-century investment technology. Professional managers are important for meeting the needs of investors and financial intermediaries but must be shown how to avoid errors and make cost-effective decisions for validation.

References

Bachelier, L. 1900. *Theorie de la speculation*. Paris: Gauthiers-Villars.

Campbell, J., A. Lo, and A.C. Mackinlay. 1997. *The Econometrics of Financial Markets*. Princeton: Princeton University Press.

Fama, E. 1970. Efficient Capital Markets: A Review of Theory and Empirical Work. *Journal of Finance* 25: 383–417.

Grossman, S., and J. Stiglitz. 1986. On the Impossibility of Informationally Efficient Markets. *American Economic Review* 70 (3): 393–408.

Lintner, John. 1965. The Valuation of Risk Assets and the Selection of Risky Investments in Stock Portfolios and Capital Budgets. *Review of Economics and Statistics* 47 (1) (February): 13–37.

Markowitz, H. 1952. Portfolio Selection. *Journal of Finance* 7 (1): 77–91.

Markowitz, H. 1956. The Optimization of a Quadratic Function Subject to Linear Constraints. *Naval Research Logistics Quarterly* 3 (1/2): 111–133.

Markowitz, H. 1959. *Portfolio Selection: Efficient Diversification of Investments*, 2nd ed. New York and Cambridge MA: Wiley and Basil Blackwell.

Menger, C. 1892. On the Origin of Money, trans. Caroline Foley. *Economic Journal* 2: 239–255.

Mossin, J. 1966. Equilibrium in a Capital Asset Market. *Econometrica* 34 (4): 768–783.

Roberts, H. 1959. Stock-Market "Patterns" and Financial Analysis: Methodological Suggestions. *Journal of Finance* 14 (1): 1–10.

Samuelson, P. 1948/1980. *Economics*, 11th ed. New York: McGraw-Hill.

Samuelson, P. 1965. Proof That Properly Anticipated Prices Fluctuate Randomly. *Industrial Management Review* 6 (2): 41–49.

Sharpe, W. 1964. Capital Asset Prices: A Theory of Market Equilibrium Under Conditions of Risk. *Journal of Finance* 19 (3) (September): 425–442.

Treynor, J. 1963. Implications for the Theory of Finance. Unpublished manuscript.

Walras, L. 1874–1877/1954. *Elements of Pure Economics, or the Theory of Social Wealth*, trans. William Jaffe from 4th ed., rev. and August ed. (1926). Homewood, IL: Irwin, 1954.

3

Rise of Institutional Quantitative Asset Management

Markowitz and CAPM theory made it possible to conceptualize and build technology to replace traditional ad hoc asset allocation and security portfolio management. The result was an explosion of technology and research in the last quarter of the twentieth century that supported the evolution of a huge industry in institutional quantitative asset management. This chapter sketches the evolution of institutional quantitative methods in equity portfolio management and asset allocation with roots beginning in the early 1970s. We first describe the CAPM-influenced framework in institutional quantitative asset management and then focus on the risk and return estimation methodologies that subsequently evolved and their rationales.[1]

---

[1] A note on the author's perspective on the rise of institutional quantitative asset management. The author graduated a PhD in mathematics from Boston University in 1971. In 1973, I began a full-time appointment at the Investment Research and Technology (IRT) Group at the Boston Company in Boston. The group, headed by Dr. Richard Crowell, an early finance PhD from MIT, included a number of highly skilled computer technologists, economists, and strategists to support their institutional clients. My role, which began as a statistical and mathematical consultant, within a year turned into an institutional quantitative analyst and strategist for the company. It was the dawn of institutional quantitative asset management. While I could not have known at the beginning of my appointment, the Boston Company IRT group was one of the world's pre-eminent investment quantitative groups with very sophisticated computer technology for its time and a policy of encouraging advanced research as part of its support for its institutional offerings.

R. O. Michaud, *Finance's Wrong Turns*, https://doi.org/10.1007/978-3-031-21863-7_3

The Institutional Asset Management Framework

Institutional quantitative equity investment strategies are typically defined in a CAPM theory "market" portfolio index-relative return framework. The investment objective is to outperform a given market benchmark by maximizing index-relative expected excess return or "alpha" relative to a given level of portfolio index-relative residual tracking error risk. The strategy can be more or less "active" depending on the desired level of tracking error from the index. The tool kit of an institutional quantitative equity portfolio manager typically includes a commercial equity risk model and a MV portfolio optimization program. Excess or expected alpha return is, by definition, beta or systematic risk-adjusted total return.

Benchmarks that define objectives may vary widely from general purpose ones such as the S&P 500 or Russell 1000 or Russell 3000, to more refined ones such as domestic small cap, growth stocks, or international. The primary limitations during the 1970s were the availability of reliable commercial equity risk models and mathematical algorithms that could MV optimize large stock universes. While optimizers were often claimed as Markowitz, actual procedures were instead often approximations based on an iterative process that nearly always converged even when the risk model was not positive semi-definite. While alternatives existed, they were less frequently used in institutional contexts.

Institutional quantitative asset allocation, in contrast, is very generally a total return efficient frontier framework. Investment convenient Markowitz MV optimizers became available relatively early in the 1970s, for generally small asset universe strategies. The procedure was often focused on financial intermediary investing such as pension funds for long-term liability asset management.

MV optimized portfolios typically included inequality constraints on asset weights. An important reason is a Regulation T requirement in the U.S., with similar regulations in most developed financial markets. As can be anticipated, sign-constrained MV optimization lives uneasily with the BC only MV optimization framework of CAPM. Theory inconsistent with practical application is a dubious route for investment success. But the hybrid framework has the virtue of practicality. It is, however, only one of several practical issues that needs to be considered as probable limitations of the success of a quantitative investment management strategy.

The Sharpe (1963) Market Line Model

MV optimization requires security and portfolio risk estimation. Equity strategy mandates often require management of hundreds or even thousands of stocks. To gain a perspective on the practical issues, suppose an MV optimization of a portfolio of hundred stocks. Theoretically, I need to estimate one hundred returns, one hundred standard deviations, and 4,950 off-diagonal correlations. Even for a small problem, the manager has a nearly herculean task of estimating MV inputs. Note also that the optimization demands even for a small set of stocks can be computationally significant.

Sharpe (1963) is one of the most influential papers of twentieth-century institutional quantitative asset management. This simple but important paper introduced the market line diagonal model as a means of simplifying the input estimation process and making MV optimization far more practical. Also of note is that the model served as a template for much of the development of quantitative equity investment technology for most of the remainder of the twentieth century.

The Sharpe market line model assumes that returns for securities are linearly related through common relationships with some factor, such as the market portfolio or index. More explicitly for each security I at time t:

$$r_{i,t} = \alpha_i + \beta_i I_t + \varepsilon_{I,t} \tag{3.1}$$

where α_i and β_i are linear parameters or coefficients of the index return I_t at time t, $\varepsilon_{i,\tau}$ is a random variable with an expected value of zero and variance ω_i. The index I may represent the return of the stock market index or some other factor thought as the most important single influence on security returns.

The return of I in period t is assumed to be determined in part by random factors:

$$I_t = \mu_I + \xi_t \tag{3.2}$$

where μ is a parameter of the return distribution of the index and ξ_t is a random variable at time t with an expected value of zero and a variance of σ_I^2 In the Sharpe model, it is assumed that the covariance $\sigma_{i,j}$ between different securities is zero for all values of i and j. In this linear model of security return, α_i and β_i relate the expected value of r_i to I. ω_i indicates the residual variance of r_i in the expected relationship 3.1. Finally, μ_I indicates the expected value of I and σ_ξ^2 the variance around that expected value.

The diagonal model requires the following predictions from a security analyst: (1) α_i, β_i, and ω_i for each of N securities and values of μ_I and σ_I^2 for the index I. The number of estimates required from the analyst is thus greatly reduced: from 5,150 to 302 for an analysis of 100 securities and from 2,003,000 to 6,002 for an analysis of 2,000 securities. Once the parameters of the diagonal model have been specified, all the inputs required for the standard portfolio analysis problem can be derived. The relationships are:

$$E(r_i) = \alpha_i + \beta_i \mu_I \quad \sigma_i^2 = \beta_i^2 \sigma_I^2$$
$$+ \omega_i^2 \quad \sigma_{i,j} = \beta_i \beta_j \sigma_I^2 \tag{3.3}$$

In this model, expected return is a linear function of the α or expected residual return of the security relative to the regression coefficient β of the security with a market index. It is essentially the simplest non-trivial model for estimating risk and return for portfolio optimization. The Sharpe single factor market model leads directly to a linear time-series regression for estimating risk-return inputs for optimization. This framework is a vast simplification of the full set of estimates required for straightforward MV portfolio optimization. Sharpe (1963) also reports that the computational time required for computing the BC only MV efficient frontier is far faster and more commercially feasible for practice.

The Sharpe (1963) diagonal model led the way to many approaches for estimating inputs for MV optimization in practice. A natural extension of the Sharpe model is to include industry and sector group indicator variables in a linear regression of the parameters with historical return data. It is also a prototype for Sharpe (1964) CAPM theory. Soon after the diagonal model becomes the CAPM security market line for estimating a security's expected return and all things center around the notion of β estimation or the notion of undiversifiable risk central to twentieth-century institutional quantitative asset management.

The Importance of Beta

It is hard to overestimate the influential impact of the Sharpe (1963) diagonal model for asset management in practice in the late twentieth century. But it is obviously far too simple a framework for actual application for an institutional investment program.

The next important step for institutional quantitative equity management evolution was the development and availability of rigorous commercial risk models initially focused on estimating beta. Commercial model services offered sophisticated econometrics and a significant data quality control process for financial management. The additional benefit is availability of security and portfolio risk measurement estimates for sponsors as well as managers for clear-channel communication.

Much of the pioneering equity risk model development was due to Barr Rosenberg. He was a smart PhD econometrician from Harvard who went on to teach at Berkeley and found his risk measurement services. He obtained a National Science Foundation (NSF) grant to build an equity risk model that became the prototype for development of his econometric methods and models for equity portfolio risk management. In 1974, Rosenberg set up Barr Rosenberg Associates, widely known as BARRA. Rosenberg became famous for promoting and distributing his "bionic" betas. He wrote a flurry of papers on econometric risk measurement for equities. His firm became synonymous with econometric equity risk modeling methods.[2] Because his NSF research was in the public domain, when portfolio risk-return estimation began to fuel quantitative institutional asset management, a number of other firms copied his methods and offered similar services.

While there are multiple variations on the theme of equity risk measurement, the original BARRA risk model is a standard template for describing many commercial risk models in practice. The BARRA beta model consists of a sophisticated linear regression of a set of descriptors in a two-step[3] generalized least squares regression framework. The regression model includes various heuristic risk factors, commonly part of traditional stock portfolio management. This multiple factor model for beta includes accounting factors such as earnings-to-price and book-price, investment factors such as earnings surprise, technical analysis factors such as return reversal, as well as industry and sector membership variables. The regressions are based on log returns and factors that generally require normalization, transformations, and weighting schemes to promote regression stability. In the BARRA model, sixty months of historical returns are used to estimate the coefficients.

---

[2] Rosenberg and McKibben (1973), Rosenberg (1974), and Rosenberg and Guy (1976a, b).

[3] The second step had to do with factor estimating residual risk from the beta regression model.

Institutional Quantitative Equity Portfolio Practice

The evolution of "beta" risk measurement included estimation of "active" or "residual" return risk, relative to a familiar benchmark such as the S&P 500 index. It became standard institutional practice to risk factor analyze a portfolio manager's portfolios estimated from commercial risk services. A manager's quarterly or semi-annual visit to a plan sponsor or endowment fund would typically include both the manager's and sponsor's discussion of performance and objectives, based on portfolio risk management analytics from a risk management service. In some cases, more than one risk management service would be used to cross check portfolio risk structure and performance consistency with agreed investment portfolio objectives for a given manager. Security and portfolio risk analytics management services remain a big business for the institutional quantitative asset management community.

A crucial next step was to introduce MV portfolio optimization based on measures of security and portfolio risk computed by risk measurement services. MV optimized portfolio management replaced traditional organizations with the new methods. MV optimization allowed managers and investors to define optimality in terms of institutional investment objectives. A manager would be selected on whether they were superior for a given objective within the sponsor's overall portfolio framework. Managers began to specialize for various investment strategies such as value, growth, international, small cap, and emerging markets. Different benchmarks defined a strategy. The manager would claim that the proposed portfolios were "optimal" relative to a given strategy or benchmark or risk objective.

Commercial risk models similar to the BARRA template have been in continuous evolution and in widespread use since the middle 1970s. They have been a very successful quantitative investment management product. These technologies were viewed as a vast improvement over the ad hoc methods that often prevailed by non-quantitative asset managers. The claimed benefit was not only security, but portfolio, risk could be measured, and various portfolio attributes could be managed and available for communication with institutional sponsors. A complete institutional quantitative investment management framework had evolved based on CAPM theoretical principles. A new era of scientific asset management practice had arrived.

While CAPM posits that a correct estimate of beta can be used to estimate security expected returns, early subscribers often expressed disappointment that the betas were not very useful on a security level. However, managers found that portfolio risk measures were often useful for discussing the risk characteristics of the portfolio in simple familiar terms for clients and sponsors. Today, there are global equity and fixed income risk models, often based on similar risk modeling frameworks. Portfolio risk characteristics are used to design and manage strategies and present results. Whether or not BARRA-type commercial factor risk models measure portfolio "risk" is arguable. The most obvious practical benefit is that they provide a way of describing the portfolio to managers, investors, and consultants in consistent investor familiar terms.

Ross APT Risk Model

The Ross (1976) Arbitrage Portfolio Theory (APT) risk model is fundamentally different from CAPM theory. Ross assumes that, in an arbitrage free capital market, securities are priced based on a linear model of systematic risk factors. In the case of no mispricing, the risk factors are systematic and affect all securities in that market. In contrast to CAPM that posits only one theoretical factor that can be estimated with many descriptors, the Ross APT model posits multiple factors that affect all the securities in an arbitrage free market. In the Ross model case, the systematic factors are conceptually more macroeconomic such as GDP growth and interest rates.

The most notable published case describing application of the APT risk model is Roll and Ross (1984). They defined four APT risk factors: inflation, industrial production, the risk premium, and the slope of the term structure. An APT risk model service was available commercially from Roll and Ross for a period of time. A fairly wide consensus of the APT model is that it is theoretically a very attractive risk framework, but the ambiguity of the relevant systematic risk factors makes the model of limited value in practice.

Fama-French Risk Model

A more recent and important alternative risk model framework is that proposed by Fama and French (FF) (1992). The original three-factor model consists of beta, size, and value as measured by book-to-market. The econometric methods used to estimate the three factors consist of long-short high-minus-low variables.[4] The objective of the procedure is to better estimate CAPM beta. It represents a serious alternative for estimating security systematic risk and expected return in a CAPM framework. The FF program is popular among academics who require a widely available data set and objective measures of security and portfolio risk for various studies of capital markets.[5] The FF framework, with modifications, has been applied to many global capital markets. Regression analyses use a good deal of long-term historical return data.

Interestingly, FF is a return to the original objective of the Rosenberg beta risk model. The FF model has often created controversy due to misinterpretation of the program. The FF factors are not designed as ways to measure expected return but distress risk. Any measure of security "risk" based on FF factors is not a current measure of active risk due to the extent of financial history being measured. Consequently, proposals to use FF factors for current active management objectives are very controversial.

Principal Component Analysis Risk Models

Principal Component Analysis (PCA) is one of the major technologies commonly used for understanding factor structure of multidimensional data.[6] A variety of factor analysis methods have been developed that have been the mainstay of social science research throughout the twentieth century.[7] Factor analysis methods may conveniently represent data and summarize the variance of many kinds of random variables. For example, measurements of physical characteristics such as head, waist, length of arm, and height for individuals can be well represented by the principal component factor "size."

PCA applications and its variants have often been applied to understanding the historical structure of capital markets with statistical procedures and associated factor analysis methods.[8] The first PCA factor for stock market data is often interpretable as a "market" index proxy. But this PCA "market" factor is not the CAPM market portfolio. It is a statistical artifact for

---

[4] Extensions include investment and profitability factors in a five-factor Fama and French (2014) model.

[5] An authoritative online database of FF factors is available from French: https://mba.tuck.dartmo uth.edu/pages/faculty/ken.french/data_library.html.

[6] Principal Component Analysis was invented by Pearson (1901).

[7] A fairly comprehensive description of traditional factor analysis methods for social science is available in Rummel (1970).

[8] Farrell, J. 1983. *Guide to Portfolio Management*, 168–174. New York: McGraw-Hill.

explaining variance for multidimensional data. The major benefit of statistical risk models from an investment perspective is parsimonious description of historical return data. Such models have had limited institutional application and acceptance. The bulk of PCA-based security and portfolio risk applications has been in international markets or specialized strategies where fundamental, accounting, or technical factor data is limited or nonexistent.[9] The price paid for data convenience is that PCA risk factors beyond a limited number of "market" or "size" factors may not be statistically significant, interpretable in a financial context, or very stable from one time period to another.

Long-Short MV Optimization

In a long-only index-relative MV optimization active management framework, the optimized portfolio will have severely limited allocations to securities representing negative alphas. Managers may often believe they have the same amount of information in negative as in positive forecasts of alpha. A long-short index-relative MV optimization framework is a theoretical solution for using negative and positive alpha information efficiently. In the classic case described in Michaud (1993), the proposal results in two long-only index-relative optimizations, one based on alpha and one based on negative alpha. The combined two-portfolio optimization fully represents positive and negative alpha information.

Such a combined long-short portfolio will require more active trading and will typically require a structured products group brokerage account. The costs of managing such a fund will be higher than a long-only portfolio. The level of portfolio management risk is greater as is always the case for leveraged strategies however carefully defined. Michaud (1993) demonstrates, under reasonable assumptions, such a strategy may be appropriate for an investor who prefers more than normal portfolio active risk to achieve more than normal active expected return. The fund theoretically has a higher Sharpe ratio for levels of risk beyond that generally available to a long-only optimized portfolio. Such a fund may be most appropriate for high-net worth investors or well-funded institutions. But such a strategy would also be more sensitive to the limitations of traditional risk models and investment technology. The issue of state-of-the-art investment theory and reliable technology is even more important in such leveraged strategies.

---

[9] A PCA "APT" software system that estimated 20 or more orthogonal stock factors has been available for multiple markets since the 1990s. See Blin and Bender (1994) and Blin et al. (1997).

The Index Fund Question

Capitalization weighted funds that mirrored various generally well-known investor indices such as the S&P 500 index began to be available for invest ment in the early 1970s. These were low-cost, highly diversified funds that replicated the "market" return as defined by the index. Such funds were a favorite of academicians who were skeptical whether actively managed funds were superior investments on a risk-adjusted cost-adjusted basis. Fund managers such as Vanguard specialized in low-cost index funds for self-advised investors.

One curious controversy emerged in the early days of index fund investing. Since all the securities in an index were bought together, there was no way to certify each asset passed an evaluation of appropriately investable. Indeed, were index funds safe for pension fund investing? But common law evolved to make the case that the investable quality of the index substituted for the need for verification of investability for each asset in the fund.[10]

In the early 1970s, index funds were not a very popular sell for many investors used to mutual fund companies promising to provide superior performance. But eventually the mantra of low cost, low risk, nearly identical market performance took hold and over time has now become a dominant part of institutional as well as retail investing.[11]

Roll (1992) Critique

In CAPM theory, the market portfolio is MV efficient. The asset management objective is to add alpha or excess portfolio return for a given level of excess risk or portfolio tracking error, relative to a market portfolio benchmark. This is the familiar institutional asset management framework of budget-constrained only index-relative portfolio optimization. The information ratio—expected index-relative excess return relative to index-relative risk level—is often considered the optimization objective of choice for active management.

Roll (1992) raised serious concerns with the index-relative portfolio optimization active management framework. His analysis noted that the objective of index-relative portfolio optimization was generally suboptimal. Unless the index is known MV efficient, all portfolios on the index-relative efficient

---

[10] https://digitalcommons.law.yale.edu/cgi/viewcontent.cgi?article=1490&context=fss_papers.

[11] In a recent text, Wigglesworth (2021) reviews many of the practical issues associated with index funds and their implications for capital markets.

frontier are suboptimal with respect to the total return MV efficient frontier. For any portfolio on the index-relative efficient frontier, there is always a portfolio with less risk and similar return or more return with similar risk than the portfolio chosen by the optimizer. Roll's study was well referenced, but his results did little to change quantitative investment management. Roll noted that perhaps estimation error and the statistical ambiguity of defining a "market" portfolio were dominating the need for a concern for absolute MV efficiency in practice. A more serious issue, which we will address in Chapter 5, is the relevance of the BC only MV portfolio optimization framework for asset management practice.

Merton's (1987) Information Cost MV Efficiency

In his presidential address, Merton (1987) describes a convenient alternative rationale for the Roll (1992) limitations of the budget-constrained index-relative MV optimization active management framework. He introduces the concept of "information cost mean variance efficiency." The notion is that a well-defined index may be considered MV efficient when information cost is considered. For example, a small cap manager may be considered MV cost efficient with respect to a small cap index. In the same way, specialist institutional managers may be viewed as information cost MV index-relative efficient. However, in practice, specialist managers may not always have a well-specified information-cost-efficient benchmark for rationalizing index-relative MV optimization. It should also be noted that the Merton assumption of BC only MV optimization framework, as will be discussed in Chapter 5, is not viable for asset management in practice.

Institutional Quantitative Return Estimation

Institutional quantitative active management requires quantitative estimates of return as well as risk. There are few universally accepted rules for professional return estimation. This is a natural consequence of the fact that the essence of hiring a professional asset manager, what the investor is paying for, is a presumptive high-quality possibly proprietary process for selecting and managing assets. For this reason, it is impossible to describe more than the popular and fairly ubiquitous frameworks for quantitative return estimation in practice during the period.[12] It should also be noted that institutional return estimation will necessarily conflict with the EMH and academic skepticism of credible added value in a cost-adjusted risk adjusted framework over investor relevant investment horizons.

Long-Term Factors and Practical Value

Investors often use the term "valuations" to refer to whether an accounting variable such as earnings-to-price or book-to-price for a stock or set of stocks is cheap or expensive relative to historical norms. Such factors are an integral part of much quantitative return estimation practice.

Table 3.1 displays six popular stock valuation factors that help illustrate the fundamental challenges for factor forecasting for stock selection in practice.[13] The six factors in the table are: (log) market cap, earnings to price, book market to price, cash earnings to price, dividend discount model return, and normalized earnings to price. The data in the table display the cross-sectional correlation of the beginning value of the indicated factor relative to the subsequent annual return of each of the six factors for 21 annual periods for monthly returns for all stocks in the Japan MSCI index for the indicated years. For example, the cross-sectional correlation of the earnings-to-price ratio for stocks in the MSCI Japan index for 1975 is 0.19. There is no adjustment for beta or risk. The averages of the correlations are tabulated at the bottom of the page with associated t-statistics.

An examination of the summary t-statistics data indicates that the size factor did not have statistically significant performance on average over the 21-year period. All the remaining five factors chosen at the beginning of the 21-year period have a summary t-stat greater than 3. The book-to-market factor had the highest t-stat over the 21-year period. But no manager would know a priori that the book-to-market factor was the most reliable one to use for valuing stocks over the period. Note that, in spite of an admirable average value t-stat over the 21-year period, it did not perform well three of the last five years and performance in 1982, 1983, and 1984 was not positive

[12] The narrative that follows for return estimation frameworks will necessarily be impacted by the author's unique experiences in actual investment practice and as a very active presenter, researcher, and participant in a number of academic and professional organizations in institutional quantitative asset management since the mid-1970s.
[13] Figure 7.1 in Michaud (1999). Originally suggested by Dr. Gary Bergstrom of Acadian Asset Management in Boston.

Table 3.1 Factor correlations in Japan with subsequent one-year total U.S. dollar return[a]

Year/Item	Market cap	Earnings to price	Book to price	Cash earnings to price	DDM	Normalized earnings to price
1975	0.22	0.19	0.14	−0.03	0.24	0.19
1976	0.11	−0.01	0.03	−0.11	0.00	−0.05
1977	0.19	0.08	0.46	0.27	−0.06	0.01
1978	0.32	−0.02	0.26	0.12	0.09	0.10
1979	−0.08	0.03	0.12	0.13	0.02	0.08
1980	−0.02	0.16	0.06	0.16	0.14	0.09
1981	−0.33	0.19	0.25	0.21	0.11	0.17
1982	−0.07	0.25	0.08	0.03	0.31	0.26
1983	0.16	0.11	0.01	−0.05	0.24	0.23
1984	−0.10	0.00	0.02	0.02	−0.09	−0.06
1985	0.08	0.06	0.25	0.12	0.01	0.08
1986	−0.13	−0.02	−0.07	−0.02	−0.14	−0.15
1987	0.19	0.12	0.26	0.13	0.13	0.20
1988	0.07	0.06	0.12	0.09	−0.06	0.07
1989	0.52	0.03	0.13	−0.03	0.00	0.05
1990	0.11	0.15	0.16	0.11	0.17	0.16
1991	0.11	−0.01	0.07	0.03	0.05	0.04
1992	0.03	−0.01	0.04	0.03	0.02	0.02
1993	−0.18	0.11	0.27	0.23	0.23	0.27
1994	0.33	−0.17	0.25	−0.07	0.05	0.14
1995	−0.12	0.21	0.07	0.13	0.18	0.19
Average	0.07	0.07	0.14	0.07	0.08	0.10
Standard deviation	0.20	0.10	0.12	0.10	0.12	0.11
t-statistic	1.56	3.32	5.27	3.13	2.96	4.13

[a]Michaud, R. 1999. *Investment Styles, Market Anomalies, and Global Stock Selection.* Research Foundation of the Chartered Financial Institute, Charlottesville

three years running. An asset manager is in danger for being fired for poor performance three years in a row.

The earnings-to-price factor would probably have been the most likely factor chosen by factor "value" managers at the beginning of the period. The factor has a large significant t-stat over the twenty-one-year period. However, there was only one good year for the six years from 1984 to 1989. A manager with only one good year out of six in a row would likely be out of business. Such historical analyses teach that, even if a factor is useful in a long-term study of stock factors, it may often be useless or even perverse over manager relevant investment horizons. The moral of this simple study is that managers and investors should be very skeptical of the investment value of academic or professional studies of statistically significant factor-return relationships over long time periods.

The Dividend Discount Model (DDM)

The interest in the 1970s of CAPM and Markowitz financial theories motivated many Wall Street and large domestic and global financial institutions to adopt more academically rigorous methods for stock valuation. The John Burr Williams (1938) model for expected return, known variously as discounted cash flow (DCF) framework, internal rate of return (IIR), or dividend discount model (DDM), became the prototype of a new wave of stock valuation methods and a significant business for a number of brokerage and consulting financial firms. The "expected return" is the estimated internal rate of return an investor would receive if purchased at the indicated price for the stream of dividends implied by a forecast of a stream of dividends by an analyst or model. The Williams framework reflected a more modern or sophisticated notion of stock value. The "intrinsic" value of a stock is not determined by whether the firm was well managed or has a history of solid earnings growth, but whether price is cheap or expensive relative to other securities in a financial market. The Williams framework became a standard for quantitative asset management for much of the 1970s and early 1980s, surviving even today in a few holdout firms.

My Wall Street career began in late 1978 as the Head of Quantitative Investment Services for a now defunct Wall Street brokerage company.[14] The Williams stock valuation framework was popularly known on Wall Street as the dividend discount model (DDM). I inherited one of the most prominent DDM stock valuation model services on the Street. In our proprietary process, the firm's research analysts were asked to provide earnings and dividend forecasts for the next 5-year periods, a computed or analyst estimated growth rate for period one and transition period two to stable conditions that were defined when the long-term growth rate and payout ratio would apply for all stocks in the research universe. The long-term growth rate and payout assumptions, standard for all stocks in the universe, were necessary to compute a geometric series estimate for terminal price, enabling computations of the internal rate of return for each stock. The firm's stock analysts had DDM technology to "manage" their intrinsic return estimates that were

---

[14] Bache, Halsey, Stuart, Shields, Inc.

presumed to include some sense of the overall market outlook provided by the research director associated with the institution. A number of accommodations had to be made particularly for growth stocks that had a policy of not issuing dividends. This is because, a stock that never pays a dividend is theoretically worthless in the Williams framework. The notion of a sustainable dividend had to be introduced to get around theoretical difficulties. Needless to say, there were many variations of the DDM framework among firms using the model for stock valuation.

The DDM is a model of total stock returns. In order to marry the DDM to the CAPM and index-relative MV portfolio optimization for quantitative investment managers, the firm's published return estimates were regressed against the beta of the stock. The result was a forecast of stock alpha that merged modern stock valuation with CAPM theory and provided the fundamental framework for institutional quantitative investment for the firm's clients and many others for much of the 1970s and 1980s.

Testing the DDM

The DDM is theoretically an attractive framework for institutional return estimation. But the DDM in practice requires many dubious assumptions about the pricing of securities in capital markets. In early 1980, I noticed a diminished lack of interest in the firm's model of estimated return by some clients. With my colleague, Paul Davis, we embarked on a program of intensive analysis of the historical performance of the proprietary model in service for a number of years for forecasting stock return. Happily, our firm had perhaps the longest continuous track record of actual use of the DDM in practice.

Our results were first presented at the American Finance Association in 1981 and published in the Journal (Michaud and Davis 1982). The paper included the results of the firm's analyst-driven proprietary model and one based on the group's use of an outside firm's analyst and earnings dividend estimates converted into a simple DDM model of stock return as a reality check for the procedure. By having more than one source of forecasts, the results could not be totally ascribed to poor analysts' forecasts in what was a successful quantitative investment service with a number of institutional clients.

Our results showed no more forecast value of the DDM returns on average than simply the current earnings-to-price ratio for the stock. We discovered what we described as an "anti-growth" stock bias for the DDM. We found that the long-term assumptions for computing the DDM returns seemed largely the source of the bias and lack of forecasting value. In a subsequent paper, Michaud (1985) demonstrated that the long-term assumptions could be used to control biases so that the valuations could be made conditional in a limited sense on the market outlook for growth or value. These two papers were influential in signaling the end of the dominance of the model for many major sell- and buy-side institutions. Interest in the DDM and such quantitative services declined fairly swiftly afterward with a few holdout institutions beyond the mid-1980s.

Multiple Valuation Models

After the limitations of the DDM framework became widely known, the seemingly obvious next step for stock valuation was to use a second, a third, or even more factors for ranking stocks and computing alphas. Why rely on only one factor when multiple factors would reduce the reliance on any one factor and the likelihood of poor performance in any one time period. This gave rise to the era of multiple valuation model (MVM) frameworks for stock valuation in institutional asset management.

As often the case in practice, the perception of a better solution to a problem often leads to excess. If a second or third factor may be useful for ranking stocks, why not use many factors? There were managers in the 1990s that used as many as fifty factors to value stocks. The question of interest was how many factors were optimal for a useful and reliable ranking of stocks relative to ex post return.

Michaud (1990) presented a simple illustration of the potential benefits and limitations of multiple factor models of return. As illustrated in Fig. 3.1, assume two factors positively correlated with ex post return with 0.2 and 0.1 correlations as in the graphic. If the factors are perfectly correlated with each other ($\rho = 1$), the relationship of some weight in one variable and the remainder in the other reflects a perfect straight-line relationship. There is no multiple valuation benefit beyond the weighted average of the correlations of the two factors. If, as is usually assumed, the two factors are not perfectly positively correlated, there can be a positive synergistic effect that provides a higher correlation with ex post return than the weighted average of the correlations, with perhaps a lower variance of return. In the case of the display, if the correlation between the two factors is zero, there is a weighting of the two factors that has greater correlation with expected return than either of the two factors. In an ideal case, two factors negatively correlated provide a possibly

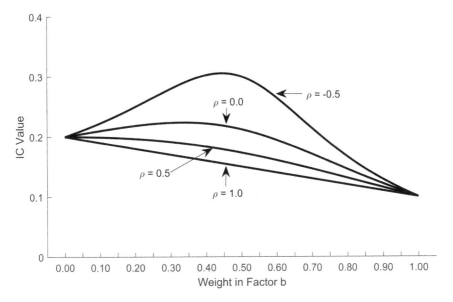

Fig. 3.1 Two-factor multiple valuation with positive predictive power (*Note* Michaud, R. 1990. "Demystifying Multiple Valuation Models." *Financial Analysts Journal* 46, no. 1: 6–8)

very significant synergistic valuation of forecast return with low variance. However, there is a downside to this scenario. We have been assuming the factors are positively correlated with ex post return. But factors can turn out to be negatively related to ex post return in any given period in practice. If, in a perverse case, both factors are negatively correlated with return, and positively synergistic, the net result could be an even more negative correlation with ex post expected return than either factor. There is no free lunch.

A Forward Test

In the 1990s, I became a member of Acadian Asset Management, a Boston-based institutional quantitative asset manager specialist in international equity markets. During my tenure, I was interested in understanding the useful factors for investing in international and U.S. capital markets. The question of what factors to use to value securities is of perennial interest in academic research and professional work. There are many philosophies, themes, and frameworks for deciding what factors to use and how to weight them.

The Michaud (1999) study of historical factor-return relationships was designed as a simple "forward test" of Acadian's actual investment experience of the efficacy of forecast factors in an ongoing institutional quantitative asset management process. The initial list of sixteen univariate factors in the study was proposed by Dr. Gary Bergstrom in 1990. The list was culled from the extant market anomaly literature and comprised most of the investment variables of practical interest in professional management at that point in time. The study was designed as to reflect a forward test, not a back test, of factor-return relationships because the factors are chosen ex ante and tested ex post. At the time the factors were proposed, there was no guarantee that any of the factors chosen ex ante would be significantly related to return ex post.

The Michaud study reported the results of the analysis of ex post return for the 1990 defined factors five and more years later. While the time period of the study is short as a test of factor-return relationships, the report included the results based on five separate stock markets—Japan, U.K., Germany, France, and the U.S. The Japan stock market had the most data available at the start of the study. It consisted of nearly 60,000 firm-months of stock factor returns. Factor analysis methods were used to understand the underlying factor structure of the sixteen variables in the data set. Seven composite investment "style" factors were defined a priori and subsequent estimates of factor-return relationships were presented for the five major global equity markets.

The results showed that from two to four composite factors were significant in one of the five capital markets. The factors that were significant varied to some extent by market. This admittedly limited study nevertheless provides a cautionary tale of the economic relevance of the academic market anomaly literature for actual investment practice. No one framework or academic published theme for investing seemed to work for all markets. There were some interesting differences between markets, suggesting financial cultural differences. A composite of the style factors for estimating ex post return was measured statistically significant. The bottom line of the study was that composites of some factors did persist as useful for estimating return over the period. However, the study strongly suggests that the process of forecasting returns requires more than a presumption of static factor relationships persisting over useful investment horizons. A sense of evolving capital markets and attention to what is, and is not, working, and why, seems essential for successful practical investment management.

Modern Statistical Estimation

Bayesian estimation is an important category of statistical methods for adding investment value in investment practice. Investment managers are naturally Bayesians. Active managers typically have a view of the market and securities within it. One of the simplest and most useful Bayesian procedures for investment in practice is Theil and Goldberger (1961).[15] The procedure is very general. In practice, an investor may often have two sources of information: historical risk-return data and analyst or strategist views. The procedure allows combining two sets of information in a statistically optimal way that reflects both the uncertainty in the data and the views under the assumptions. It is a simple but often valuable tool for the analyst as a quantitative feedback framework for understanding uncertainty in the data and rationalizing views.

Michaud and Michaud (2008, Ch. 8) describe some shrinkage estimates of return and risk that can be useful for reducing the impact of outlier data in historical risk-return estimates in portfolio optimization. Any historical return data set will have outlier data that are unlikely to repeat in a future time period. Stein and similar shrinkage methods are often useful in forecasting. Like many statistical procedures, they tend to work best with a sufficient amount of historical and diverse data. But there is no free lunch. The shrinkage method tradeoff is that some of the return character or risk structure of the data is necessarily shrunk to the prior in the procedure with generally unknown level of reliability.

Hensel et al. (1991) and the Manager Irrelevance Fallacy

Institutional asset allocation policy is the long-term average of asset weights in the asset allocation portfolio. Asset allocation policy is often referred to as the single most important investment decision an investor can make and the bedrock of a well-defined investment program.[16]

The notion of the primacy of the asset allocation decision for investment is based on a widely referenced study by Brinson et al. (1986). They report that 94% of the variance of the performance of institutionally managed portfolios can be ascribed simply to the long-term average of asset weights, or investment policy, of the asset allocation portfolio. The study was very influential

---

[15] See also Theil (1971, 347–352).
[16] Sharpe and Tint (1990).

because it was the first out-of-sample analysis of the performance of institutional pension fund managers. Not only was investment policy primary
but portfolio active management and security selection were essentially irrelevant. They also reported that investment policy was well approximated by
the stock/bond ratio of the fund.

The concept of the primacy of asset allocation policy persists to this day.
There is only one little problem with the mantra. The Brinson study is in
error. Hensel et al. (1991) repeated the Brinson (1986) study using the only
other database of actual historical institutional fund manager performance.
As in Brinson, the results were not a back test but the actual long-term
performance of institutional pension fund managers. Hensel et al. noted that
the definition of "investment policy" used in the Brinson study was essentially an estimate of performance relative to the riskless rate of return. Such
a measure of performance cannot be considered a valid performance measure
of investment policy. They corrected the measure of investment policy
return as return relative to the average return of the institutional managers.
With this correction, they found that asset allocation policy was roughly
attributable to 40% of the variance of return, fund selection attributable
to 40%, and fund management 20%[17]—a strikingly different result and
message for asset management practice. The important conclusion is that
institutional asset management is not irrelevant. All components of successful
asset allocation portfolio management—systematic risk policy (stock/bond
ratio), portfolio management (portfolio construction, rebalancing, trading),
and fund selection—are as likely to be as important as any other.

Given that the Hensel et al. study was published shortly after Brinson and
in the same Journal, why were the Hensel teachings ignored for many years,
even up to the present time, by academics and professionals alike? The answer
to this question says a great deal about the actual workings of the investment
community and its reliance on consultants and academics. It is hard to escape
the conclusion that partisans of a simple truth benefited at the expense of
more relevant and effective investment principles. Understanding such issues
is highly relevant for defining best practices in financial education.

Institutional Active Management Status

By the late 1990s, institutional quantitative active management had evolved
to a very sophisticated level of professionalism, especially in terms of risk

---

[17] Given the statistical limitations of the study, all three components are roughly equally likely
important.

measurement. It was a far cry from traditional stock picking managers relying on intuition and focusing on small segments of capital markets. But the level of sophistication was often not reflected in superior risk-adjusted, cost-adjusted reliable investment performance, relative to more traditional benchmarks. As we will show in Chapter 5, this is because the theory and tools were deficient in sometimes subtle but fundamental ways. No amount of data and computational technical wizardry could repair the shaky foundation it had been built on. The rise of low-cost passive management was a challenge no level of sophistication easily could hide from or ignore.

References

Blin, J., and S. Bender. 1994. Arbitrage and the Structure of Risk: A Mathematical Analysis. Working Paper, APT, Inc.

Blin, J., S. Bender, and J.B. Guerard, Jr. 1997. Earnings Forecasts, Revisions and Momentum in the Estimation of Efficient Market-Neutral Japanese and U.S. Portfolios. In *Research in Finance*, ed. A. Chen, 15. Greenwich, CT: JAI Press.

Brinson, G., L.R. Hood, and G. Beebower. 1986. Determinants of Portfolio Performance. *Financial Analyst Journal* 42 (4): 39–44.

Fama, E.F., and K.R. French. 1992. The Cross-Section of Expected Stock Returns. *Journal of Finance* 47 (2): 427–446.

Fama, E.F., and K.R. French. 2014. A Five-Factor Asset Pricing Model. *Journal of Financial Economics* 116: 1–22.

Hensel, C., D. Ezra, and J. Ilkiw. 1991. The Importance of the Asset Allocation Decision. *Financial Analyst Journal* (July–August).

Merton, R.C. 1987. *Journal of Finance* 42 (3): 483–510.

Michaud, R. 1985. A Scenario-Dependent Dividend Discount Model: Bridging the Gap Betbetween Top-down Investment Information and Bottom-up Forecasts. *Financial Analysts Journal* 41 (6): 49–59.

Michaud, R. 1990. Demystifying Multiple Valuation Models. *Financial Analysts Journal* 46 (1): 6–8.

Michaud, R. 1993. Are Long-Short Equity Strategies Superior? *Financial Analyst Journal* 49 (6): 44–49.

Michaud, R. 1999. *Investment Styles, Market Anomalies, and Global Stock Selection*. Charlottesville: Research Foundation of the Chartered Financial Institute.

Michaud, R., and P. Davis 1982. Valuation Model Bias and the Scale Structure of Dividend Discount Returns. *Journal of Finance* 37 (2): 563–573.

Michaud, R., and R. Michaud. 2008. *Efficient Asset Management: A Practical Guide to Stock Portfolio Optimization and Asset Allocation*. New York: Oxford University Press. 1st ed. 1998, originally published by Harvard Business School Press, Boston.

Pearson, K. 1901. On Lines and Planes of Closest Fit to Systems of Points in Space. *Philosophical Magazine* 2 (11): 559–572.

Roll, R. 1992. A Mean/Variance Analysis of Tracking Error. *Journal of Portfolio Management* 18 (4) (Summer): 13–22.

Roll, R., and Stephen Ross. 1984. On the Cross-Sectional Relation Between Expected Returns and Betas. *Journal of Finance* 49 (March): 101–121.

Rosenberg, B. 1974. Extra-Market Components of Covariance in Security Returns. *Journal of Financial and Quantitative Analysis* 9 (March): 263–274.

Rosenberg, B., and W. McKibben. 1973. The Prediction of Systematic and Specific Risk in Common Stocks. *Journal of Financial and Quantitative Analysis* 8 (3): 317–334.

Rosenberg, B., and J. Guy. 1976a. Prediction of Beta from Investment Fundamentals: Part One. *Financial Analyst Journal* 32 (3): 60–72.

Rosenberg, B., and J. Guy. 1976b. *Prediction of Beta from Investment Fundamentals: Part Two* 32 (4): 62–70.

Ross, S. 1976. The Arbitrage Theory of Capital Asset Pricing. *Journal of Economic Theory* 13 (3) (December): 341–360.

Rummel, R.J. 1970. *Applied Factor Analysis*. Evanston: Northwestern University Press.

Sharpe, W. 1963. A Simplified Model for Portfolio Analysis. *Management Science* 9 (2): 277–293.

Sharpe, W. 1964. Capital Asset Prices: A Theory of Market Equilibrium Under Conditions of Risk. *Journal of Finance* 19 (3) (September): 425–442.

Sharpe, W., and L. Tint. 1990. Liabilities—A New Approach. *The Journal of Portfolio Management* 16 (2): 5–10.

Theil, H. 1971. *Principles of Econometrics*. New York: Wiley.

Theil, H., and A.S. Goldberger. 1961. On Pure and Mixed Statistical Estimation in Economics. *International Economic Review* 2: 65–78.

Wigglesworth, R. 2021. *Trillions*. London: Penguin Group.

Williams, J.B. 1938. *Theory of Investment Value*. Cambridge, MA: Harvard University Press.

4

Finance Theory in Crisis

Since the middle of the twentieth century, the Sharpe (1964) Lintner (1965) capital asset pricing model (CAPM) has been the dominant theoretical framework of modern finance. CAPM is based on von Neumann-Morgenstern (VM) (1944) expected utility theory, the normative and descriptive model for rational decision making under uncertainty that has defined modern economics and much of social science since mid-century. The Markowitz (1952a) behavioral axioms that resulted in the invention of the Markowitz frontier are not dependent of VM rationality or CAPM theory. Markowitz (1952b) also raised concerns that wealth level and gains and loss behavior central to finance were limitations of VM expected utility theory. But the nature of systems of rational axioms, largely ignored by expected utility theorists, has deep roots in the work of mathematical logical systems and paradoxes in early twentieth century that have significant relevance to modern social science. Notably, sociological norms also proposed in Durkheim and Keynes as alternative frameworks for rational financial behavior were largely dismissed by economic theorists. But fundamental axiomatic critiques of VM rationality theory have emerged in the middle and late twentieth century in the work of Allais (1953, 1988), Kahneman and Tversky (1979), Tversky and Kahneman (1992) and many others. The same critiques apply to much of economic theory and psychological theory, the two social sciences most concerned with rational individual choice behavior. As we will show, flawed axiomatic theories of rational

© The Author(s), under exclusive license to Springer Nature
Switzerland AG 2023
R. O. Michaud, *Finance's Wrong Turns*,
https://doi.org/10.1007/978-3-031-21863-7_4

investor behavior can provide a convincing rationale for ineffective institutional quantitative asset management practice and axiomatic frameworks for rational preference theory.[1]

CAPM Theory Redux

The Sharpe (1964) CAPM is a beautifully written and mathematically rigorous theoretical framework given its assumptions. This is the paper that formally launched neoclassical twentieth-century financial theory and motivated development of the paradigms that became institutional quantitative asset management in practice. Our discussion here focuses on CAPM assumptions as presented in Chapter 2.

Sharpe's objective is on deriving the price of risk from investor preferences. He invokes VM expected utility theory as the framework of choice for rational decision making under uncertainty. In order to connect with the Markowitz MV efficient frontier framework, he assumes that investor's expected utility can be approximated by a quadratic utility function. In order to develop a theory of equilibrium in capital markets, he further assumes a common pure rate of interest, with all investors able to borrow or lend funds on equal terms and homogeneous investor expectations. Sharpe is also assuming budget-constrained MV optimization for analytical convenience. Long-only portfolio MV optimization is not considered.

Critiques of the CAPM have often focused on the lack of realism implied by the capital market equilibrium assumptions on investment practice. While valid this is not our concern. Equilibrium theoretical assumptions are often made to derive key results. Our focus instead is on evidence that CAPM theory fundamentally does not admit of a realization for effective asset management practice due to the VM axiomatic framework and budget-constrained only MV optimization assumptions. We first address the implications of the VM axioms here and defer discussion of the quadratic utility preference function to Chapter 5.

---

[1] Alternative critiques of neoclassical finance theory from a biological perspective include Farmer and Lo (1999) and Lo (2004).

VM Rationality Framework

The Sharpe assumption that each investor is a VM game theory axiom rational agent is the key to understanding of twentieth-century neoclassical finance, economics, and much research in mathematical psychology. VM axioms provide a highly plausible set of mathematically sophisticated axioms for characterizing rigorous "rational" decision making under uncertainty. Von Neumann was one of the greatest mathematical minds of the twentieth century. The VM axioms are extraordinarily sophisticated and a well-respected rationality framework with many applications for decision making in the context of well-defined repeatable games. But the modern theory of decision making under uncertainty came from a logical analysis of games rather than psychological analysis of individual behavior. The theory represented a normative model more of an idealized rational decision maker rather than a description of consistent informed behavior of real people in situations of uncertainty.

Actual human investment behavior in financial markets is not trivially consistent with a repeatable game framework. In a repeatable game such as roulette in a casino, while the outcome of each spin of the wheel is uncertain, the probability of a win for the casino is stable and positive. Assuming the roulette wheel is operating properly, the game will lead to a positive predictable outcome for the casino on average over many plays of the game. Interestingly, a roulette game framework has often been used to rationalize an investment strategy.

In contrast, in the play of an investment game, the probability of a positive investment outcome is not an objectively measurable parameter. An investor's assessment of the probability of a win of the investment game is not comparable to the objectively observable probability of winning for the casino.

Savage (1954) provides an important extension of VM axioms that includes the concept of personal probability assessments. Savage shows that even if an investor's assessment of the "probability of winning" may not be objectively observable it can be viewed as following a set of rules that are consistent with VM rationality axiomatization. The influential Savage extension of VM rationality axioms in finance, economics, and psychology posited that the behavior of a social agent may be consistent with the hyper rationality of a VM game theory decision maker. In this context, the Sharpe (1964) presumption of VM rationality is theoretically rationalizable.

The Allais Paradox

The first serious crack in the credibility of VM-Savage axioms as a basis for rational decision making for investing was published by Allais (1953). Maurice Allais was a polymath. He made fundamental contributions in a number of scientific fields and won a Nobel Prize in economics in 1988. In the much studied Allais paradox, investors are asked to choose a sequence of two bets that they prefer.

Step 1:   You are asked to choose either A1 or B1.
           A1 $1 mill 100% prob
           B1 $1 mill 89% prob $0 mill 1% prob, $5 mill 10% prob
Which one would you choose?

Step 2:   You are then asked to choose either A2 or B2.
           A2 $0 89% prob $1 mill 11% prob
           B2 $0 90% prob $5 mill 10% prob
Which one would you choose?

The Allais gambles have been tested many times. Most subjects choose A1 and B2. Subjects choose A1 because they prefer $1 million dollars for certain over the small possibility of getting nothing even though they may end up with $5 million dollars. In the second case, subjects choose B2 because winning nothing is very probable, but there is a probability of gaining $5 million instead of $1 million with about the same probability.

As it turns out, if you choose A1 and are VM-Savage rational, you should also choose A2 and vice versa according to VM game theory axioms. This may seem odd at first. To show why it's true, let's redefine the gambles without changing their value.

Step 1:   Choose either:
           A1 $1 mil 89% prob, $1 mil 1% prob, $1 mil 10% prob
           B1 $1 mil 89% prob, $0 mil 1% prob, $5 mil 10% prob

Step 2:   Choose either:
           A2 $0 mil 89% prob $1 mil 1% prob, $1 mil 10% prob
           B2 $0 mil 89% prob $0 mil 1% prob, $5 mil 10% prob

Or   equivalently:
           A1 $1 mil 1% prob, $1 mil 10% prob
           B1 $0 mil 1% prob, $5 mil 10% prob

Step 2:   Choose either:

A2	$1 mil 1% prob,	$1 mil 10% prob
B2	$0 mil 1% prob,	$5 mil 10% prob

After elimination of redundancy, A1 and A2 both have the same probability of winning $1 million while B1 and B2 both have the same probability of winning $5 million. Therefore, it is formally correct that the choice of the two gambles A1 vs B1 and A2 vs B2 are the same. So if you chose A1 you should choose A2 and vice versa. Humans must be crazy right? Even when individuals are shown the deconstruction of the gambles, they often still prefer choosing A1 and B2. What is happening?

The Allais paradox illustrates a critical flaw in the VM axiomatization of rational decision making under uncertainty. Allais demonstrates that human behavior can be inconsistent with VM axioms in the presence of high and low probability events with significant payoffs. In the first gamble, humans tend to focus on the certainty of winning 1 million dollars as opposed to the possibility of winning 5 million dollars relative to the possibility of losing everything. In the second case, the much lower probability of winning 1 million dollars is not as attractive as almost the same probability of winning 5 million dollars. Investors are switching preference rules without regard to axiomatic precepts.

This seemingly benign set of gambles is no toy example. It is informed by a deep understanding of how humans behave in the presence of very low probability events with excessive utility.[2] At the time few American financial economists were convinced of the seriousness of the issue. However, as Paul Samuelson noted on the occasion of Allais being awarded a Nobel Prize in economics in 1988, two years before the one awarded to Markowitz and Sharpe: "Had Allais' earliest writings been in English, a generation of economic theory would have taken a different course."[3]

In an interesting side note, Savage found himself in Paris in 1952 at a conference with Allais.[4] Allais challenged him to consider his paradox. To his embarrassment, Savage answered inconsistent with VM axioms. When he realized what he had done, he commented: "Oh, but I made a mistake. Obviously, the right answer is the expected utility solution." Was Savage making

---

[2] Allais surely was aware of Pascal's (1935) wager and its implicit critique to VM axiom theory. See further Archie (2006).

[3] Lohr, S. 1988. "A French Economist Wins Nobel." *New York Times*.

[4] Reported in Orléan (2014, pp. 312–317).

a mistake or was it consistent with actual human decision making in uncertainty? The VM axioms make sense for many kinds of games, but are they valid for humans? This issue was not definitively resolved in the minds of many working social scientists until twenty-five years later.

Kahneman and Tversky Gains and Losses

Kahneman and Tversky (KT) (1979) were psychologists studying human decision making under uncertainty. Mathematical psychology at that time was largely based on VM axiom expected utility theory. Following Markowitz (1952b), KT performed extensive psychological experiments of human decision making focusing on gains and loss behavior. They documented that humans are consistently more averse to losses than preserving similar gains. In simple terms, if you have $100, you are much more averse of losing $100 or even $50 than valuing gaining another $100. As illustrated in Fig. 4.1, they demonstrate that human utility functions consistently have a kink at the loss vs gains point. This implies, as Allais had shown years earlier, no utility function that is consistent with VM axioms can consistently describe human decision making under uncertainty. Their further research on prospect theory (Tversky and Kahneman 1992) led to a Nobel Prize in economics in 2002 for Kahneman. Unfortunately, by that time, Tversky was deceased.

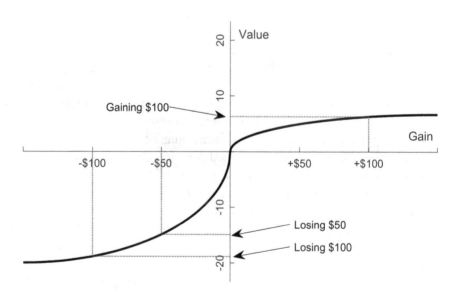

Fig. 4.1   Kahneman-Tversky kinked utility function

My interpretation of the Allais and KT experiments is that the human decision process switches rational "utility" gears under certain conditions when presented with highly uncertain bets. The utility function gear switch can in no way be modeled in VM axiom theory. In the first Allais case, a small gain versus a significant loss indicates a traditional concave upward sloping preference function of $1 million for sure while in the second case faced with little to lose investors tend to switch to reduced aversion to risk "utility" function.

The Allais and KT results were demonstrations that cast new light on a deeper understanding of how humans deal with uncertainty in great generality as well as for investment. But if the VM axioms are not consistent with human decision making, why not? The VM axiom assumptions in Sharpe (1964) and CAPM is no simple blunder but a deeply fundamental flaw for defining rational human decision making that had, in fact, been noted years earlier. The crux of the matter is whether any axiom system, not just VM game theory, can ever be used to represent consistent human rational decision making.

Roots in the 1930s Crisis in Mathematics

It is appropriate to consider research in consistent formal logical systems that were the precursor to VM game theory rationality. It is not very well known outside of mathematical communities, and often forgotten in contemporary times, that mathematics in the early twentieth century had a severe crisis of confidence in the use of axiom systems as a means of guiding rational decisions. While mathematics was being applied to great success in physics, engineering, and many other scientific fields, mathematicians themselves began to wonder how they could be sure that their proofs were valid and did not have any hidden flaws. Mathematical proofs, after all, are just another human activity with many examples of sometimes persistent errors from thousands of years of mathematical thought.

Do mathematical proofs represent absolute truths? Euclid's axioms for geometry are considered a gold standard of mathematical rigor and often said to represent absolute truth. However, Euclid's axioms are not useful as a theory for any other than the geometry of a flat surface. In contrast, calculus, invented independently by Fermat, Newton, and Leibniz in the middle of the seventeenth century, was necessary to solve real practical problems in physics. But a rigorous foundation for calculus was not established, despite several attempts, for more than 150 years. Cauchy (1821), in a text considered one of the most influential in all mathematical history, provided a workable definition of limits and a means to make them the basis of a rigorous theory of calculus. Cauchy also revitalized the idea that all mathematics should be set on rigorous foundations. Peano (1889) is revered for his highly formal mathematical rigor of number theoretical axioms by avoiding language and intuition.

For many logicians and mathematicians, the idea of removing error in human reasoning led to the notion of banishing intuition in proofs. Frege, a great late nineteenth-century logician, proposed that all mathematical thought be put into formal symbolic logic expressions. Frege (1893) spent his working life to write all mathematics and set theory into symbolic logical arguments. But his effort was not successful. Russell (1903) noted a serious flaw in his system.[5] It is known as Russell's paradox: The set of all sets is not a member of itself. It is the familiar paradox: I am lying. If I am lying then I am telling the truth and if I am telling the truth I am lying. Alfred North Whitehead and Bertrand Russell wrote their famous *Principia Mathematica* (1910, 1912, 1913) which proposed to write all of mathematics in terms of formal symbolic logical deductions devoid of the Russell paradox and all known logical paradoxes. But the Principia, in an important sense, was a dead end, at least to mathematicians. It solved the logical paradox only by appropriation.

Mathematicians preferred to base logical deduction on explicit axioms for derivation of correct proofs. In the early twentieth century, David Hilbert was widely acknowledged as among the greatest of working mathematicians. His widely praised work on geometry went well beyond Euclid in terms of logical abstraction.[6] In the Hilbert and Bernays's (1934) *Grundlagen*, the authors set themselves the task of axiomatically systematizing all of mathematics. Hilbert said: "A proof must be given for each branch of mathematics that the permitted procedures of demonstration can never yield A and not A." Hilbert was from Konigsberg in Germany. Ironically, a twenty-five-year-old mathematician also from Konigsberg was going to completely destroy Hilbert's aspiration.

Kurt Gödel (1931) published his famous incompleteness theorem. A consistent axiom system is one where it is not possible to prove A and not A from the axioms. Gödel proved that any consistent axiom system large enough to include numbers was necessarily incomplete. Including numbers

---

[5] In a letter to Frege.
[6] Hilbert (1980 [1899]).

seems a minimal condition for a set of axioms for mathematical thought.[7] Gödel's theorem means that there are always things that are true but can't be proved from a consistent set of axioms if the axioms include numbers.

Gödel's theorem is a momentous event in twentieth-century thought and human intellectual history. Gödel had shown that try as he might Hilbert, or anyone else, would never be able to prove all of mathematics was consistent even for something as simple as a theory for numbers. This was an intellectual earthquake of the first order. Hilbert and Bernays wrote two editions of their Grundlagen. The second edition included discussion of Gödel's theorem. Hilbert became very depressed and skeptical about the prospects of the consistency of mathematical thought. He never did any more research in mathematics afterward.

Gödel's incompleteness theorems were in the Zeitgeist. Church (1936) was also independently proving theorems similar to Gödel at Michigan. In addition, Turing (1936), who was defining the concept of the universal machine, also found analogous Gödel theory properties in the behavior of logical machines in the form of computability and the halting problem.

Resolutions

The amazing achievements of Gödel (1931), Church (1936), and Turing (1936) left many elite mathematicians in a state similar to a nervous breakdown. How confident could mathematicians be that there was not some fundamental flaw in many or even all of mathematical proofs? At that time, a group of mostly French mathematicians took the fictitious name "Bourbaki" and proposed to rewrite all of mathematics in rigorous axiomatic set theory terms. In a famous speech in 1948 to the Association for Symbolic Logic and in an article in "L'Architecture des Mathematicques," Bourbaki proposed the "working mathematician" philosophical framework.[8] Bourbaki explains their philosophical foundation in simple terms: Axioms do not define human rationality; rationality defines the axioms that are to be used for some particular purpose. When inconsistencies arise, we change the axioms or we add axioms to explain the new concept. It is always, no more or less, than just another

---

[7] Note that Euclidean geometry has no notion of a metric.
[8] "Foundations of Mathematics for the Working Mathematician," *Journal of Symbolic Logic*, 14 (1949): 1–8; "L'Architecture des Mathématicques," in *Les Grand Courants de la Pensée Mathématicques* (Paris, 1948, ed. F. Le Lionnais, pp. 33–47.

problem to be solved. The history of the crisis in mathematics and its reso-lutions in the early and mid-twentieth century ranks as one of the all-time greatest achievements in the history of human intellectual achievement.

Consilience

The word "consilience" denotes the existence of a transcendent unity asso-ciated with multiple sources of knowledge. It represents a point in time where multiple proofs may indicate a single reliable truth. From the Markowitz (1952a, b) axioms, Allais (1953, 1988) examples of inconsis-tent axiomatic rational thought, Kahneman and Tversky (1979), and Tversky and Kahneman (1992) illustration of VM utility inconsistent gains and loss behavior, Gödel (1931), Church (1936), and Turing (1936) proofs of the limitations of consistent logical axiom systems, Bourbaki's (1948, 49) simple working mathematician philosophical principles, are also consistent (as we will show in Chapter 8) with Knight (1921) and Keynes (1936). All point to a single fundamental truth on the nature of human consciousness and rational decision making under uncertainty. How Bourbaki proposes to resolve the crisis in mathematics is the same solution the twenty-five-year-old Harry Markowitz used to found financial theory in the Chicago Business Library: scientific truth as axioms of the consistent behavior of informed agents for a given purpose. CAPM and VM-Savage theory do not describe a valid theory of finance for practice. For investment decision making, VM-Savage theory represents an invalid understanding of human rationality in practice. It also points, as Bourbaki explains, to a fundamental set of principles for understanding all rational informed human decision making, with or without uncertainty.

There is an important footnote to this intellectual history of trying to systematize human rationality. There are other sets of rational axioms—Quiggin (1982, 1993) and Michaud et al. (2020)—that are consistent with Allais (1953, 1988) and Tversky and Kahneman (1992).[9] In both cases, the authors start with behavior first and then find axioms that characterize the behavior, as proposed by Bourbaki. Such proposals can't claim that all rational human decision-making behavior under uncertainty can be explained by their axioms. This is because of Gödel-type incompleteness theorems. But they can claim that known rational behavior is likely systematizable with consistent rational axioms.

---

[9] In an important event, Quiggin (1982) rank-dependent expected utility innovation is a fundamental component of Tversky and Kahneman (1992) cumulative prospect theory.

Conclusion

These momentous events in the history of science in the twentieth century, and our evolving understanding of rational human decision making under uncertainty, reflects a fundamental error in modern finance and economics in its reliance on the VM axioms for defining human rational decision making. It is also a ubiquitous intellectual error well beyond finance. The effort to ascribe hyper-rational logical principles as a framework for defining "correct" human decisions is transcendent in many branches of social sciences and human endeavors. Although it has appeared in most of human history, it may be called the fundamental error of rational decision making discovered in the twentieth century: The consistency of a logical axiom system does not necessarily imply human truth.[10] We need an investor decision making oriented theory to support a theoretical framework for investment management in practice. The consequence for finance but also for much of social science, and indeed for human thought, is profound. Note that Hume (1748) is highly prescient: There are fundamental limits to human understanding and theory that can never be definitive as an explanation of reality. Should music theory define beauty in music? Should art theory define beauty in art? Should Marxist theory define human social welfare? In all these cases and in many others, it is a matter of the intellectual cart having been placed in front of the human horse.

References

Allais, M. 1953. Le comportement de l'homme rationnel devant le risque: Critique des postulats et axioms de l'école Americaine. *Econometrica* 21 (4): 503–546.

Allais, M. 1988. The General Theory of Random Choices in Relation to the Invariant Cardinal Utility Function and the Specific Probability Function. In *Risk, Decision and Rationality*, ed. B. Munier, 233–289. Dordrecht: Reidel.

Archie, L.C. 2006. Blaise Pascal, 'Pascal's Wager'. *Philosophy of Religion* (June 26).

Bourbaki. 1948. L'Architecture des Mathematicques. In *Les Grand Courants de la Pensée Mathématicques*, ed. F. Le Lionnais, 33–47. Paris.

Bourbaki, N. 1949. Foundations of Mathematics for the Working Mathematician. *Journal of Symbolic Logic* 14: 1–8.

Cauchy, A. 1821. Cours D'Analyse de L'Ecole Royales Polytechnique. Librarie du Roi et de la Bibliotheque du Roi, Paris.

---

[10] It seems worth noting that the resolution Bourbaki (1948, 1949) proposed for mathematics was published four years after publication of the VM (1944) game theory axioms.

Church, A. 1936. An Unsolvable Problem of Elementary Number Theory. *American Journal of Mathematics* 58 (2): 345–363.

Farmer, J., and A. Lo. 1999. Frontiers of Finance: Evolution and Efficient Markets. *Proceedings of the National Academy of Sciences of the United States of America* 96 (18): 9991–9992.

Frege, G. 1893/1903. Grundgesetze der Arithmetik, begriffsschriftlich abgeleitet (2 volumes: Jena, 1893, 1903).

Gödel, K. 1931. Uber formal unentscheid Satze der Principia Mathematica und verwandter Systeme, I. Trans: On Formally Undecidable Propositions of Principia Mathematica and Related Systems I. Monash. *Mathematical Physics* 38: 173–198.

Hilbert, D. 1980 (1899). *Grundlagen de Geometrie*, 2nd ed. Chicago: Open Court.

Hilbert, D.P. 1934 (1938). Bernays. *Grundlagen der Mathematik* (2 volumes; Berlin).

Hume, D. 1748. *An Enquiry Concerning Human Understanding*. London: Oxford.

Kahneman, D., and A. Tversky. 1979. Prospect Theory: An Analysis of Decision Under Risk. *Econometrica* 47 (2): 263–291.

Keynes, J. 1936. *The General Theory of Employment, Interest, and Money, Economics*. London: Macmillan and Co.

Knight, F. 1921. *Risk, Uncertainty, and Profit*. Boston: Houghton Mifflin Company.

Lintner, John. 1965. The Valuation of Risk Assets and the Selection of Risky Investments in Stock Portfolios and Capital Budgets. *Review of Economics and Statistics* 47 (1) (February): 13–37.

Lo, A. 2004. Adaptive Markets Hypothesis. *The Journal of Portfolio Management* 30 (5): 15–29.

Markowitz, H. 1952a. Portfolio Selection. *Journal of Finance* 7 (1): 77–91.

Markowitz, H. 1952b. Utility of Wealth. *Journal of Political Economy* 60 (2): 151–158.

Michaud, R., D. Esch, and R. Michaud. 2020. Estimation Error and the Fundamental Law of Active Management: Is Quant Fundamentally Flawed. *Journal of Investing* 29 (4): 20–30.

Orléan, A. 2014. *The Empire of Value*. Cambridge: MIT Press.

Quiggin, J. 1982. A Theory of Anticipated Utility. *Journal of Economic Behavior and Organization* 3 (4): 323–343.

Quiggin, J. 1993. *Generalized Expected Utility Theory: The Rank-Dependent Model*. London: Kluwer Academic Publishers.

Pascal, B. 1935. *Pensées et Opuscule Philosophique*. Paris: Librarie Hachette.

Peano, G. 1889. *Arithmetices principia, nova methodo exposita*. Torino: Bocca.

Russell, B.D. 1903. Letter to Frege. In *Principles of Mathematics*. Cambridge.

Savage, L.J. 1954. *Foundations of Statistics*. NY: Wiley.

Sharpe, W. 1964. Capital Asset Prices: A Theory of Market Equilibrium Under Conditions of Risk. *Journal of Finance* 19 (3) (September): 425–442.

Turing, A. 1936. On Computable Numbers, with an Applications to the Entscheidungsproblem. *Proceedings of the London Mathematical Society* 42 (1): 230–265.

Tversky, A., and D. Kahneman. 1992. Advances in Prospect Theory: Cumulative Representation of Uncertainty. *Journal of Risk and Uncertainty* 5: 297–323.

Von Neumann, J., and O. Morgenstern. 1944. *Theory of Games and Economic Behavior*. Princeton: Princeton University Press.

Whitehead, A.N., and B. Russell. 1910 (1912–1913). *Principia Mathematica*, vols. 1, 2, 3. Cambridge: Cambridge University Press.

5

The Crisis at the Workbench

Markowitz (1952, 1959) represents a milestone in modern finance. Markowitz theory has defined the fundamental notion of portfolio optimality for social science and provides a detailed proposal for rational institutional asset management in practice. But the quadratic programming optimization framework underlying Markowitz theory is an application of operations research technology. When implemented using an electronic computer with realistic financial data, it often fails as a practical tool for portfolio management. This failure—a fundamental misunderstanding of the limitations of statistically estimated information—has been largely ignored or misunderstood for more than thirty years (Michaud 1989). The central problem is a mismatch between the endemic uncertainty represented by financial data and that assumed in applications of linear programming technology. We introduce multivariate normal distribution Monte Carlo simulation as a means to understand the limitations of classical portfolio optimality and to develop a more effective theoretical framework for practice.

Markowitz Optimization as the Institutional Standard

Markowitz MV optimization has been the theoretical institutional standard of choice for defining portfolio optimization for more than sixty years. It is theoretically correct given correct inputs under the assumptions. It provides

© The Author(s), under exclusive license to Springer Nature
Switzerland AG 2023
R. O. Michaud, *Finance's Wrong Turns*,
https://doi.org/10.1007/978-3-031-21863-7_5

the promise of optimally diversified portfolios. Unlike many single-point proposals for constructing optimal portfolios, the Markowitz frontier allows for a wide spectrum of optimal investment strategies at various risk levels. Commercial asset allocators and optimizers are nearly all based on versions of Markowitz MV optimization.

In inventing the MV efficient frontier, Markowitz was confronted with the analytically difficult problem of minimizing the variance of portfolio return, subject to a given level of estimated portfolio return of an inequality-constrained portfolio. In a long-only portfolio, asset weightings are constrained to be between 0 and 1. Calculus, as used in the derivation of CAPM theory, was not a viable procedure. The Markowitz (1952) epiphany was to recognize that parametric quadratic programming was a mathematical computational framework that allowed for optimization of the MV of return, subject to budget and sign constraints. Markowitz (1955, 1959) invented the Critical Line Algorithm (CLA) that enables efficient computation of budget- and inequality-constrained MV optimized portfolios. At the time of its invention, quadratic programming was the only viable computational framework for defining linear constrained MV optimized portfolios.

Strategies in Widespread Practice

In 1974, at the beginning of my career in institutional asset management, the director of the quant group asked me to develop a Markowitz optimized European country market mutual fund portfolio. The company hired a consultant in European capital markets and appropriated suitable international capital market data for analysis. At that time, few in asset management had seen a correctly computed Markowitz MV optimized portfolio for an institutionally relevant asset allocation problem.[1] When I presented my optimization results, the director of the quant group, looking over my printout, noted a thirty-three percent allocation to the Austrian market. He asked if this was an error. It was not. But this was obviously an absurd investment result for the company. The impractical character of the solutions from the Markowitz MV optimizer ended the project. I learned a surprising fact: A theoretically correct Markowitz optimal portfolio may not be commercially viable for institutional asset management.[2] I also learned to be very skeptical of the practical benefits of even the most illustrious tools in asset management.

---

[1] We used the MIT-Rand quadratic programming routine originally developed by Markowitz.

[2] See Michaud and Michaud (2008a) for further discussion.

A Simple Example

To illustrate the practical investment issues associated with Markowitz MV optimization, we define a straightforward asset allocation example consistent with much current practice. We chose five Vanguard bond indices—short-term government, intermediate-term government, long-term government, inflation-protection, and high-yield corporate—and eight Vanguard equity and real estate indices—large cap value, large cap growth, small cap value, small cap growth, European, Pacific, emerging markets, and real estate. We used monthly historical price returns from Yahoo for the twenty-year period from January 2001 to December 2020. The annualized CPI-adjusted monthly returns comprise the risk-return inputs for a Markowitz (sign- and sum-to-one constrained) MV optimization. The Markowitz MV efficient frontier and the mean and standard deviation of the assets are shown in Fig. 5.1.

The display shows that the fixed income indices plot low and to the left of the risk spectrum while equities and real estate plot generally above and to the right. Note that small cap growth had the highest mean return while emerging markets reflect the most risk. Neither large cap value, Pacific, nor European indices performed well, relative to available alternatives during this period. On the other hand, long-term bonds were a strong performer relative to risk. All indices had a positive average return over the twenty-year period.

The data set and period are designed to illustrate the result of a MV asset allocation that may mirror contemporary professional asset allocation.

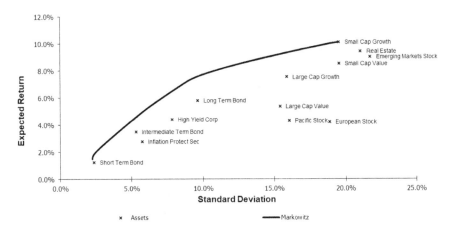

Fig. 5.1 Markowitz Mean–Variance efficient frontier: Vanguard equity/fixed income indices annualized monthly returns 1/2000–12/2020

From first principles, the Markowitz efficient frontier seems to be reasonably consistent with investment intuition over this historical period. If so, why would Michaud (1989) report that investment professionals typically avoid using a pure Markowitz optimized portfolio for asset management? The following analysis provides a simple explanation of the problems often encountered in practice.

Figure 5.2 describes the results of the MV optimized asset allocation in a color-coded composition map. The optimal asset allocations are graphed for each of one hundred portfolios on the efficient frontier from low to high risk. The left side of the display presents the assets included at the bottom, or minimum variance optimized portfolios, on the efficient frontier. The right side of the display presents the maximum optimized portfolio on the efficient frontier. The Figure shows how assets enter and leave the optimized portfolios for different levels of risk. The composition map indicates that assets populating the efficient frontier: short-term government in red, intermediate government in red–orange, long-term government in orange, small cap growth in cyan, real estate in blue in the bottom corner, and small slivers of high-yield corporate bonds and large cap growth at low risk in yellow and green. The Appendix at the end of the chapter provides some specific values for the asset allocations across the risk spectrum.

From an investment perspective, thirteen assets were considered important, but only five are significant in most of the frontier, and only two or three

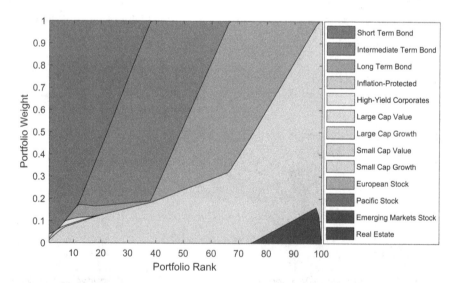

Fig. 5.2 Markowitz optimization portfolio composition map: Vanguard equity/fixed income indices annualized monthly returns 1/2000–12/2020

define optimality over most of the important central spectrum of risk. Also note the choppiness of the optimized portfolios where asset entrances and exits can result from even small changes in risk levels. This instability can raise serious difficulties when working with a client to define an appropriate level of portfolio risk where small shifts in risk level can lead to large shifts in allocations. Faced with such difficulties, it is no wonder that managers will manage the results by introducing various ad hoc constraints and proposed changes in estimates. While few asset managers use pure historical return data to develop an institutional quality asset allocation in practice, such risk-return estimates are not investment irrelevant and not "in error," but are typical examples of the difficulties associated with using MV optimized portfolios in practice.

Operations Research and Investment Management

The basis of the Markowitz optimization procedure, parametric quadratic programming, is an operations research procedure. It is an extension of linear programming methods. Such applications typically assume great precision of information such as in physics experiments, engineering, rocketry, communication, and construction. This is why modern electronic computers are designed to have, as a minimum, the IEEE[3] standard of sixteen decimal places of accuracy for storing data. This standard has been set to enable reliable computational applications essential to contemporary science and modern society.

But data and information for financial management are different. A ten percent forecast of return for the S&P 500 index goes into the computer with fourteen trailing zeros. That's a lot of certainty as a forecast of a stock market index that has a roughly twenty percent annualized monthly return standard deviation. While it is patently absurd in most cases in practice to think of sixteen decimal place accuracy forecasts of the return of financial securities, the computational reality is that the quadratic programming optimizer assumes all estimates accurate to sixteen decimal places. This includes not only return and risk estimates for each asset in the optimization, but also the many correlations between assets representing the underlying risk structure of the portfolio.

---

[3] Institute of Electrical and Electronics Engineers.

The mismatch between the ambiguity of much financial information and the precision power of the quadratic programming algorithm in an electronic computer results in a great deal of instability and ambiguity for defining a MV optimized portfolio. It is the reason why Markowitz optimized portfolios are known to be highly sensitive to what seems, from an investment point of view, like very small changes in risk-return estimates. The optimization tends to over emphasize assets with large returns, small standard deviations, and small or negative correlations while under emphasizing assets with small returns, large standard deviations, and large correlations. As Michaud (1989) noted, the inherent instability of the Markowitz procedure tends to act as an "error maximizer." The result is that the notion of optimality is highly ambiguous. Which of the many possible optimized portfolios within the range of estimation error of the inputs is likely to be the "optimal" portfolio? MV optimized portfolios often make little if any investment sense to experienced investors and often perform poorly out-of-sample.

Demonstrating MV Optimization Instability

Jobson and Korkie (JK) (1981) were the first to apply rigorous Monte Carlo simulation methods to measure the out-of-sample average performance of MV portfolio optimization. Their simple but important pioneering study inaugurated a new class of methods that has had the potential for revolutionizing quantitative asset management and financial theory. The important difference in their case, relative to Fig. 5.2, is that the MV optimization is BC only. A note about BC only MV optimization. Unlike Markowitz linear constrained MV optimization, the procedure in JK is represented by a simple analytical formula:

$$X = \overset{-1}{\Sigma} \mu \left/ \left(\mathbf{1}' \overset{-1}{\Sigma} \mu \right) \right. \tag{5.1}$$

where

Σ	the covariance matrix
Σ^{-1}	inverse of the covariance matrix
μ	column vector of estimated returns
X	column vector of optimal weights
1	column vector of ones with length equal to the number of assets

The formula computes a single sum-to-one maximum Sharpe ratio (MSR) MV optimal portfolio on the BC only MV efficient frontier. It is precisely the same portfolio that maximizes the quadratic utility function approximation of expected utility assumed in Sharpe (1964) CAPM theory. The formula or quadratic function approximation of expected utility is often used as a convenient approximation of Markowitz MV optimization when no inequality constraints are included. It is also ubiquitous in twentieth-century economics and mathematical frameworks of human rational behavior. As we will show, it can rightly be considered the seed of the fundamental limitations of financial theory in the twentieth century and beyond and of the ineffectiveness of much institutional quantitative asset management technology and investment strategies.

With this background, we proceed to describe the simulation procedure in the JK study:

A referee is assumed to know the means, standard deviations, and correlations of twenty stocks estimated from historical monthly returns from the Toronto Stock Exchange. Step 1: Compute the Sharpe ratio (SR) of the max Sharpe ratio (MSR) portfolio on the BC only MV efficient frontier for the referee's data. Step 2: Monte Carlo simulate sixty vectors assuming a multivariate normal distribution of returns for the twenty stocks in the optimization universe. Each sixty vectors of return represent five years of monthly simulated historical data. Compute means, standard deviations, and correlations for the sixty months of simulated multinormal returns for the twenty stocks. Compute the value of the SR of the simulated MSR portfolio with the referee's risk-return data. Step 3: Repeat step 2 many times. Step 4: Compute the average of the SRs for the referee's data for the many simulated MSR optimal portfolios. Compute the equal-weighted portfolio SR for the referee's data. Compare the results: referee data SR 0.32, equal weighted SR 0.27, average simulated SR 0.08.

The average out-of-sample simulated SRs of BC only MV optimized portfolios is dramatically inferior to the actual SR of the referee's data and almost as inferior as the SR of simple equal weighting. JK concludes that BC only MV optimization has little, if any, investment value in practice.

Comment on the JK Simulation Framework

A simulation study, as in JK, is a rigorous statistical-mathematical proof of the out-of-sample average performance of a procedure under the assumptions. It is entirely analogous to a rigorous proof of a mathematical theorem for a given set of data. The results of both are conditional of the assumptions. In a simulation proof, the conditions need to be "realistic" to be useful in applications. This is why most professional or academic publications require actual historical data in illustrations.

In the JK experiment, it is possible to reduce the underperformance of the MV optimized portfolios by changing some of the assumptions. For example, simulating one hundred instead of sixty returns to compute the simulated MV inputs, also examined in JK, reduces the observed underperformance of BC only optimized portfolios relative to the referee's data.[4] This is because increasing the number of simulated returns for computing the simulated MV efficient frontier inputs decreases the variance of the average of the simulated SRs and consequently increases the level of information assumed in input estimates. But more simulated data are no panacea. It only results in more similarity to the referee's assumptions in the referee's in-sample MV frontier portfolio. The referee's truth is in no way guaranteed to reflect the relevant risk-return parameters in the actual out-of-sample period. It is at best a useful fiction to help understand the characteristics of the optimization process. In addition, it also requires that the return generation process over a much longer historical period is stable and can remain relevant as an estimate for the out-of-sample investment period.

The sixty months assumption for computing inputs in an optimization is arguably similar to that used in the regressions of many commercial services for estimating security and portfolio risk. A different data set will lead to quantitatively different but often similar qualitative results. While a larger optimization universe can impact the results when compared to equal weighting, it is also true that more securities in the optimization may result in more estimation error in the MV optimization. For small optimization universes as in asset allocation application, given the magnitude of the disparities measured in the experiment, we can safely conclude that BC MV optimization should generally be considered of little if any investment value in practice.

Fundamental Implications of the JK Experiment

The JK experiment has transcendent implications for contemporary financial theory and many applications in contemporary institutional asset management. CAPM theory assumes quadratic function expected utility preference

---

[4] Michaud and Michaud (2008a, Ch. 4) examine alternative assumptions in the JK simulation framework.

which is precisely the BC only MV optimization framework in formula 5.1 under the assumptions. This means that the twentieth-century standard for financial theory and much of institutional asset management reflects a framework that has little, if any, investment value for asset management in investment practice, the presumptive rationale for the theory. In neoclassical CAPM theory, the definition of portfolio optimality is central. If the CAPM framework is no more reliably investment effective than security selection, concepts such as beta as a measure of systematic risk, market portfolio as MV efficient, or the definition of alpha as the objective of an investment strategy are unlikely useful or recommendable for defining investment strategies or implementation in asset management.[5]

Due to the influence of CAPM theory, the BC only MV optimizer for designing investment strategies or building investment technology has been widespread in institutional management since the mid-twentieth century. The analytical convenience of the formula for MV optimization has dominated considerations of investment effectiveness. This has happened often.

Black-Litterman Optimization

A very popular application of BC only MV optimization is Black-Litterman (BL) (Black and Litterman 1992). BL claim their algorithm solves the instability and ambiguity of Markowitz MV optimization. Because the procedure is an application of BC only MV optimization, the procedure produces a single MSR optimal portfolio. The procedure also requires the assumption of a "market" portfolio in equilibrium and investor active asset allocation views. Due to the lack of linear inequality constraints, the BL optimized portfolio often results in an undesirably large leveraged and/or short allocations. BL introduce an ad hoc "tau" parameter to mix the computed MSR optimized portfolio with the assumed market portfolio to compute more desirable solutions such as a sign-constrained MV optimal portfolio. In the case that the resulting tau-adjusted portfolio is sign constrained, Michaud et al. (2013) demonstrate that Markowitz MV optimization provides the identical solution

---

[5] It is important to note that this flawed framework for asset management assumed in the foundational construction of the CAPM was based on widespread economic theory prevalent at that time. As Dixit (2012) summarizing Samuelson's legacy to modern economics notes: "Samuelson's interest in consumer theory began early – perhaps the most important article is 1938 a [1966] – and continued throughout his life. It occupies a central place in Foundations; three full chapters and many sections of other chapters are devoted to it. Using the framework of maximizing an ordinal utility function subject to a budget constraint, Samuelson derives many meaningful theorems, …".

under identical assumptions, while providing an efficient frontier of relevant optimized alternatives. The result is that the procedure fails to improve the limitations of Markowltz MV optimization. If the tau adjusted portfolio is not sign constrained, it is heir to the serious investment limitations demonstrated in the JK simulation study. Essentially, BL optimization fails its objectives and is not recommendable in practice.

Out-of-Sample Linear Constrained MV Optimization

Frost and Savarino (FS) (1988) is an iconic Monte Carlo simulation study that addresses the importance of inequality constraints on out-of-sample average performance of Markowitz MV optimized portfolios. The simulation experiment for a 200-stock optimization universe focused on long-only MV optimized portfolios that included an unrestricted case plus an additional five max security constraint strategies—5%, 2%, 1%, 2/3 of 1%, ½ of 1%—for three levels of investor risk aversion. The results showed that simulated out-of-sample average performance tended to increase by imposing more severe constraints on asset weights in the optimization up to a point. This is because optimizers tend to overweight securities with more estimation error and underweight securities with less.

The FS results provide an important rationale for the quantitative manager practice of including sign and ad hoc constraints to MV optimized portfolios. The constraints avoid the limitations of estimation error in MV optimization by moderating the impact of the corner portfolios characteristic of Markowitz optimization. While the motivation for including constraints may often concern improving marketing acceptability of the optimized portfolios for clients, the FS results indicate that managers were well advised to do so as well from an out-of-sample performance perspective.[6]

Information Level, Universe Size, and the Fundamental Law

Michaud et al. (2020) document a series of reports based on the investment unreliable Formula 5.1 as a basis for defining institutional quantitative investment strategies. The Michaud et al.'s study also provides a convenient

---

[6] Michaud (1989) describes some of the "aesthetic" behavior of portfolio optimization asset managers.

generalization of the JK and FS simulation results under various assumptions. The report focuses on the limitations of the out-of-sample value of popular institutional investment practices based on BC only MV optimization derived from Grinold (1989) theory and popularized in Grinold and Kahn (1999) and Clarke de Silva and Thorley (2002, 2006).

The "IC" or information correlation represents the amount of information or correlation in a forecast of the out-of-sample mean return on average in the simulation study. The IC is a standard used in equity portfolio management representing levels of information in an institutional quantitative asset manager's forecast of ex post returns. Different IC levels can be represented by different numbers of simulated returns in computing the MV inputs.

Michaud et al. (2020) document the average out-of-sample performance of equal weighting, budget-constrained, and long-only MV optimization for stock universes that range from five to five hundred in size, for IC values of 0.10, 0.20, and 0.30. The study is based on a recent history of U.S. publicly available market data (1994–2013) of all stocks from the largest 1000 in market capitalization with contiguous data from the period with some investability exclusions, resulting in 544 stocks that met our criteria. An IC value of 0.10 is widely assumed an aspirational standard in applications for the information level in an active manager's investment strategy. A key assumption of the Michaud et al.'s study is that the IC does not vary as the size of the optimization universe varies. This critical assumption is implemented with a novel resampling without replacement procedure. The purpose of the constant IC assumption imbedded in the simulation design is to give the strategies a fair test for adding investment value as a function of increasing the size of the optimization universe. We also include the implications of the positive IC without estimation error as a function of optimization universe size that is the basis of Grinold's (1989) active management theory.

The results of these simulation studies are displayed in Fig. 5.3. The exhibit reports the simulated average out-of-sample SR for the indicated strategy as a function of the size of the optimization universe for IC = 0.10 level for different optimization assumptions. In the case of small optimization universes, typical in asset allocation studies, at the left-hand side of the display, the results are consistent with the JK findings that an "equal-weight" strategy can be superior to MV optimization. The results are also consistent with those in FS of the superiority of sign-constrained portfolios (blue curve) relative to BC MV optimized (cyan) portfolios.[7] Linear inequality constraints can add strikingly beneficial value to a well-defined MV

---

[7] Simulations take increasing computer time for increasing size of the optimization universe.

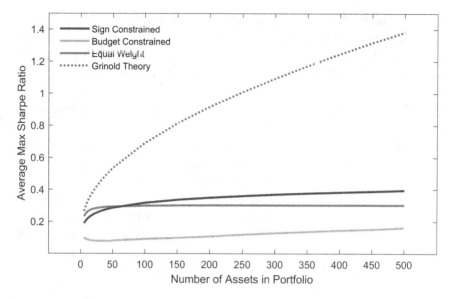

Fig. 5.3 Max sharpe ratios: 5 to 500 asset optimization universe, IC = 0.1* (Taken from Michaud, Richard O., David N. Esch, and Robert O. Michaud. 2020. Estimation error and the fundamental law of active management: is quant fundamentally flawed? *The Journal of Investing* 29 [4]: 20–30)

optimized portfolio. The importance of these results is particularly significant for many contemporary institutional asset management strategies where proposals for adding investment value by simply adding securities to the optimization universe, adding factors to forecast return, trading more frequently, or reducing constraints are based on the BC only MV optimization framework and very likely ineffective or self-defeating. Finally, Fig. 5.3 displays the highly unrealistic average SR level claimed according to the no estimation error BC only MV optimization theory that underlies the Grinold (1989) Law.

Markowitz's Revenge

The results of our simulations are a strikingly positive statement for rationalizing the investment value of the sign constraint originally proposed in Markowitz MV optimization. There is a remarkable difference between the out-of-sample investment value of "sign-constrained" versus "budget-constrained" only MV optimization, across the entire spectrum of optimization universe size in the study. This is a serious indictment of academic studies of the widespread presumption that the analytical Formula 5.1 is in any way a valid approximation of Markowitz MV optimization. Other simulation assumptions that the BC MV optimization outperforming sign constrained are likely highly unrealistic for practice.[8] Not only because of real-world issues such as costs of trading, or of information level assumed constant with universe size, but also a required manager information level considered highly aspirational in the industry. In practice, size and information level, beyond some reasonable point, are likely negatively correlated, implying that the BC curve in Fig. 5.3 likely declines beyond some size point.

It is remarkable how persistent equal weighting is superior even for relatively large optimization universes for the assumed IC level of 0.1. It is also interesting to note that sign-constrained optimization can be inferior to equal weight for small optimization universes under the assumptions.

The display results are most dramatic comparing the no estimation error theoretical SR level in BC MV optimization-based Grinold (1989) theory relative to simulated actual average SR values. The theory is highly unrealistic and no reliable guide for investment practice. The implications of the result should be taken very seriously considering that Grinold theory is the basis of many "sophisticated" quantitative investments programs particularly at the institutional investment level, in use today.

The Role of the Market Portfolio in Theory and Practice

A central concept and cornerstone in CAPM and much of twentieth-century institutional investment technology and practice are the centrality of the "Market" for portfolio optimization. Markowitz (2005) published an ingenious "triangle" proof to show that the market portfolio is not and can't be MV efficient, contradicting a basic tenet in equilibrium CAPM theory. The corollary is that CAPM theory is invalid as a framework for asset management in practice. The important consequence for asset management is that the institutional framework of index-relative MV optimization is necessarily suboptimal. While Roll (1992) published a similar critique of the suboptimality of index-relative MV optimization, the proof was limited due to assuming budget-constrained only MV optimization. Strangely, few seemed to notice or appreciate the importance of this simple masterpiece of early

---

[8] Michaud et al. (2020) also examine additional presumptive IC levels. The level of information required to overcome the limitations of budget-constrained only MV optimization appears highly unlikely in practice on any sustainable level.

twenty-first-century financial theory. We summarize the proof and discuss its implications for asset management.

Assume Markowitz MV portfolio optimization of a long-only portfolio for three assets with allocations X1, X2, and X3 = 1 − X1 − X2. All possible locations of the three assets are in a triangle from the origin to 1 on the x axis, from the origin to 1 on the y axis, and within the line from (0,1) to (1,0) (ignoring the value of X3). Mean-variance return inputs given for all three securities define the locus of the Markowitz MV efficient frontier. There are three investors A, B, C with different levels of risk aversion, where we assume at least one investor on each of the two branches of a three asset MV efficient frontier. Compute the minimum variance portfolio and plot inside the triangle in terms of the x and y axes (ignoring X3). Compute the MV efficient portfolios for the three investors MVA, MVB, and MVC from lowest to highest return on the MV efficient frontier. Plot the MVA optimal portfolio in x and y axes in the triangle. There is a line that starts from the min variance portfolio to MVA and continues to until it hits the 0 value for y at the x axis $(x_1,0)$ (for the given inputs) which is the first critical point on the MV efficient frontier. MVB is at $(x_2,0)$ on the segment from $(0,0)$ to $(x_1,0)$. All possible remaining portfolios on the MV efficient frontier must now remain on the line segment from $(x_2,0)$ to the origin. The maximum return MVC efficient portfolio is a single asset and must reside at the origin.

Now compute the market portfolio which is an average of all the MV efficient portfolios for the three investors. Where is it? An average is inside a triangle from MVA to MVB to MVC. The market portfolio is by construction not on the MV efficient frontier and can't be MV efficient. No MV efficient investor invests in the market portfolio.

It follows that the conclusions of the CAPM are invalid. If the market portfolio is not MV efficient, if no investor invests in the market portfolio, then beta is not a measure of undiversifiable return and alpha is not a measure of active return, CAPM is not a realizable theory for asset management in practice. The proof is entirely generalizable.

There is a sense of frustration in the Markowitz (2005) title of his paper.[9] This may reflect the fact that the results contradicting a market portfolio-based CAPM theory for investment practice had been published twice before (Markowitz 1987; Markowitz and Todd 2000) with little notice or attention in the financial community. Remarkably, in hindsight, given that the Markowitz frontier is concave, this result was implicit in Markowitz (1952) nearly seventy years ago.

---

[9] "A theoretical distinction and so what?".

Summary

For more than sixty years, classical financial theory and many publications of MV optimization have ignored the need for including the inequality constraint assumption in Markowitz (1952). The history of the ignorance or dismissal of the JK results suggests a profound blindness of convenience in academic teaching and of editors, reviewers, and publishers of research and texts in modern finance.[10]

The most important general conclusion is the lack of investment value of the BC MV optimization assumption, used in a preponderance of academic and professional journal research articles and texts on optimization, in finance and social science theory. The CAPM-based Grinold Law and its strategic implications are highly unlikely to be a useful guide in asset management practice. BC MV optimization is not a good approximation to Markowitz theory. Markowitz linear constrained MV optimization is superior and essential for theory and as a realistic and relevant framework for asset management. The simulation results coupled with the warnings in Markowitz (2005) provide a serious critique of the relevance of CAPM-based finance theory and institutional investment frameworks for why asset management in practice has often been deficient.

Appendix

Markowitz optimized efficient frontier allocations: Vanguard thirteen indices 1/2001–12/2020

Assets	Portfolio number					
	1	21	41	61	81	100
Short Term Bond	96.0%	53.9%	0.0%	0.0%	0.0%	0.0%
Intermediate Term Bond	0.0%	29.2%	72.7%	15.5%	0.0%	0.0%
Long Term Bond	0.0%	3.9%	7.6%	55.1%	37.7%	0.0%
Inflation Protect Sec	0.0%	0.0%	0.0%	0.0%	0.0%	0.0%
High Yield Corp	0.0%	0.0%	0.0%	0.0%	0.0%	0.0%
Large Cap Value	2.0%	0.0%	0.0%	0.0%	0.0%	0.0%
Large Cap Growth	0.7%	0.0%	0.0%	0.0%	0.0%	0.0%
Small Cap Value	0.0%	0.0%	0.0%	0.0%	0.0%	0.0%
Small Cap Growth	1.3%	13.0%	19.7%	29.4%	57.8%	100.0%

(continued)

---

[10] This is a serious indictment of the status of editorship and the reviewing process of even the most respected academic and professional journals in finance today.

(continued)

Assets	Portfolio number					
	1	21	41	61	81	100
European Stock	0.0%	0.0%	0.0%	0.0%	0.0%	0.0%
Pacific Stock	0.0%	0.0%	0.0%	0.0%	0.0%	0.0%
Emerging Markets Stock	0.0%	0.0%	0.0%	0.0%	0.0%	0.0%
Real Estate	0.0%	0.0%	0.0%	0.0%	4.5%	0.0%

The display documents the Markowitz MV efficient frontier asset allocations from minimum variance in the first column to maximum estimated return in the last column with four intermediate risk levels from left to right associated with Fig. 5.2

References

Black, F., and R. Litterman. 1992. Global Portfolio Optimization. *Financial Analysts Journal* 48 (5): 28–43.

Clarke, R., H. deSilva, and S. Thorley. 2002. Portfolio Constraints and the Fundamental Law of Active Management. *Financial Analysts Journal* 58 (5): 48–66.

Clarke, R., H. deSilva, and S. Thorley. 2006. The Fundamental Law of Active Portfolio Management. *Journal of Investment Management* 4 (3): 54–72.

Dixit, A. 2012. Paul Samuelson's Legacy. *Annual Reviews of Economics* 4: 1–31.

Frost, P., and J. Savarino. 1988. For Better Performance: Constrain Portfolio Weights. *Journal of Portfolio Management* 15 (1): 29–34.

Grinold, R. 1989. The Fundamental Law of Active Management. *Journal of Portfolio Management* 15 (3): 30–37.

Grinold, R., and R. Kahn. 1999. *Active Portfolio Management*, 2nd ed. New York: McGraw-Hill.

Jobson, D., and B. Korkie. 1981. Putting Markowitz Theory to Work. *Journal of Portfolio Management* 7 (4): 70–74.

Markowitz, H. 1952. Portfolio Selection. *Journal of Finance* 7 (1): 77–91.

Markowitz, H. 1955. The Optimization of a Quadratic Function Subject to Linear Constraints. *Naval Research Logistics Quarterly* 3: 111–133.

Markowitz, H. 1959. *Portfolio Selection: Efficient Diversification of Investments*, 2nd ed. New York and Cambridge, MA: Wiley and Basil Blackwell.

Markowitz, H. 1987. *Mean-Variance Analysis in Portfolio Choice and Capital Markets*. New Hope, Pennsylvania: Fabozzi Associates.

Markowitz, H. 2005. Market Efficiency: A Theoretical Distinction and So What? *Financial Analysts Journal* 61 (5): 17–30.

Markowitz, H., and G.G. Todd. 2000. *Mean-Variance Analysis in Portfolio Choice and Capital Markets*. New Jersey: John Wiley & Sons.

Michaud, R. 1989. The Markowitz Optimization Enigma: Is Optimized Optimal? *Financial Analysts Journal* 45 (1) (January–February): 31–42.

Michaud, R., and R. Michaud. 2008a. *Efficient Asset Management: A Practical Guide to Stock Portfolio Optimization and Asset Allocation.* New York: Oxford University Press. 1st ed. 1998, originally published by Harvard Business School Press, Boston.

Michaud, R., and R. Michaud. 2008b. Estimation Error and Portfolio Optimization: A Resampling Solution. *Journal of Investment Management* 6 (1): 8–28.

Michaud, R., D. Esch, and R. Michaud. 2013. Deconstructing Black-Litterman: How to Get the Portfolio You Already Knew You Wanted. *Journal of Investment Management* 11 (1): 6–20.

Michaud, R., D. Esch, and R. Michaud. 2020. Estimation Error and the Fundamental Law of Asset Management: Is Quant Fundamentally Flaawed? *Journal of Investing* 29 (4): 20–30.

Roll, R. 1992. A Mean/Variance Analysis of Tracking Error. *Journal of Portfolio Management* 18 (4) (Summer): 13–22.

Sharpe, W. 1964. Capital Asset Prices: A Theory of Market Equilibrium Under Conditions of Risk. *Journal of Finance* 19 (3) (September): 425–442.

6

The Michaud Efficient Frontier and Expected Utility

No man ever steps in the same river twice.

Heraclitus of Ephesus c. 500 B.C.

In spite of its critical limitations, Markowitz MV optimization remains the framework of choice for defining portfolio optimality in much contemporary practice. This is because many managers naturally think in terms of MV estimates for securities and MV portfolio optimality. However, due to instability of the procedure, practical implementation requires many interventions that often limit any real additive value, as we observed in our example of an asset allocation optimization in Chapter 5. In this chapter, we introduce an innovation based on Monte Carlo multivariate normal return estimation that is designed to resolve the limitations of Markowitz linear constrained MV optimization in practice. The essential result is the invention of the Michaud efficient frontier (Michaud 1998), which transforms the Markowitz operations research algorithm into multivariate statistical estimation in a Markowitz MV efficient frontier framework.[1] We will also show that the new procedure can be interpreted as investor expected utility estimation for Markowitz optimization.

---

[1] Michaud (1998, Ch. 6). Invented by Richard Michaud and Robert Michaud U.S patent #6003008.

Instability in Markowitz MV Optimization

The endemic instability and ambiguity of Markowitz MV optimization can be illustrated with the use of Monte Carlo multivariate normal return simulation. The historical data and case described in Fig. 5.1 are the basis of the illustration. Specifically, Monte Carlo simulates twenty years of monthly CPI-adjusted returns based on the historical return data in Fig. 5.1, assuming a multivariate normal return distribution. Given a simulated set of twenty-year returns, compute the resulting risk-return inputs and associated sign and BC Markowitz MV efficient frontier. The simulation can be repeated multiple times. In Fig. 6.1, the original efficient frontier associated with the historical data is graphed in black and twenty-five simulated MV efficient frontiers are displayed in cyan. While simulation studies for constructing efficient portfolios may often consist of thousands of simulated MV efficient frontiers, in this case only a small number are shown for pedagogical purposes.

By definition, each simulated Markowitz MV efficient frontier in Fig. 6.1 is based on the same data as in Fig. 5.1. By definition, any simulated efficient frontier is, from a statistical perspective, as optimal as any other. Note some MV simulated frontiers reflect far more expected return than the original Markowitz frontier, others much less; some indicate more risk than the classic frontier, others less. The simulated frontiers may often result in investment

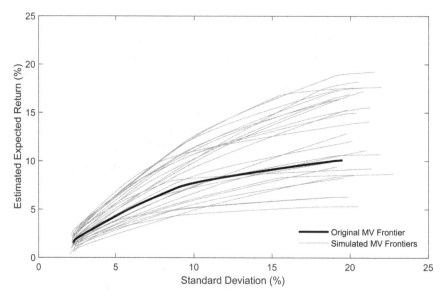

Fig. 6.1 Original and Monte Carlo simulation MV frontiers: Thirteen Vanguard indices: 1\2001–12\2020

scenarios with exotic properties that may be interpretable as the consequence of fashionable risk measures. The problem of ambiguity is as serious as instability. Which efficient frontier from any of these equally optimal ones to choose? Presentations of these results to informed investment professionals and noted academics have often elicited concerned comments as to how anyone can manage money with this level of instability in a MV efficient frontier-based investment process.

Figure 6.1 should impress any financial economist of the endemic instability of Markowitz MV optimization who may have considered the frontier a valuable representation of investment information. However, an even starker presentation of MV optimization instability can be demonstrated. Consider the 60/40 stock/bond ratio MV optimized portfolio on the Markowitz efficient frontier in Fig. 6.1. Monte Carlo multinormal simulates the 60/40 portfolio by resampling the risk returns for 240 monthly returns and plot the resulting simulated optimal portfolio in terms of the referee's data. Figure 6.2 presents the results of this experiment. As can be observed, the simulated MV optimal 60/40 portfolios, all as statistically optimal as the original, are scattered across nearly the entire MV efficient frontier. In fact, the simulated portfolios hardly resemble the original position and are often far from the 60/40 point on the frontier. In light of the presentation, given how often 60/40 portfolios are computed by the investment community for a wide range of applications, it does not seem extreme to say that Markowitz MV optimization has little, if any, investment value even for sign-constrained portfolios.

From one perspective, the instability of MV efficiency with estimation error may indicate little hope of practical investment value. However, our simulations suggest a multivariate statistical estimation route to transform MV optimization into a far more investment useful procedure. A natural notion for resolving the instability investment limitations of Markowitz MV optimized portfolios is to average the simulated MV efficient frontiers in Fig. 6.1. But how to define a procedure appropriate for averaging MV efficient frontiers? The key is to return to the iconic Markowitz (1952) question: How do investors think?

Min and Max Michaud Efficient Portfolios

Consider a highly risk-averse investor faced with the simulated efficient frontiers in Fig. 6.1. In this case, the minimum variance portfolio is the optimal portfolio for any given simulated MV efficient frontier. Since all

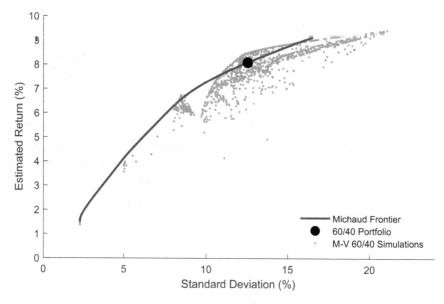

Fig. 6.2 Simulated Markowitz 60/40 MV optimal portfolios

simulated efficient frontiers are equally likely optimal by definition, the statistically appropriate estimate of the minimum variance optimal portfolio is the average of the portfolio weights of all the simulated minimum variance portfolios. This will be the minimum variance portfolio on the proposed new Michaud MV efficient frontier.

Now consider a risk indifferent investor. The maximum return portfolio is the optimal portfolio for any given simulated efficient frontier. Since all simulated maximum return portfolios are equally likely optimal, the statistically appropriate estimate of the maximum return portfolio is the average of the portfolio weights of all the simulated maximum return portfolios. This will be the maximum return portfolio on the new Michaud frontier. The process for averaging the simulated efficient frontiers between the min and max efficient frontiers requires more discussion.

The Equal-Return-Rank (ERR) Algorithm

To compute statistically appropriate averages of MV efficient portfolios between proposed min and max Michaud efficient portfolios requires the introduction of the equal-return-rank algorithm (ERR). In this procedure, compute N equal-return-ranked efficient portfolios for each simulated MV efficient frontier in Fig. 6.1. Compute the average portfolio weight for each

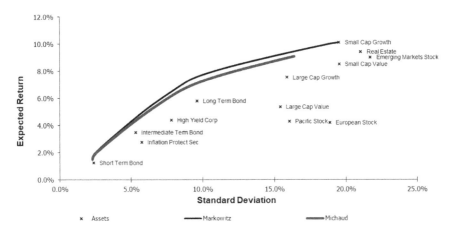

Fig. 6.3 Markowitz and Michaud efficient frontiers: Thirteen Vanguard indices 1/2001–12/2020

of the N-ranked MV efficient frontier portfolios. The averages of the N-ranked MV efficient portfolios provide a practical and useful approximation to the theoretical continuous Michaud MV efficient frontier further discussed below. In many applications, computing 100-rank efficient portfolios is often sufficient for most applications of practical interest.

Figure 6.3 displays the Markowitz and Michaud MV efficient frontiers for the monthly return data in Fig. 5.1 using the ERR algorithm in the Michaud case for 100 ERR MV optimized portfolios. The Michaud frontier plots below and shifted to the left of Markowitz in-sample by averaging many Markowitz efficient frontiers and reducing susceptibility to outlier unlikely risk-return estimates. The Michaud frontier does not increase estimated return but is designed to provide a more stable and investment unambiguous definition of portfolio optimality.

The Michaud Frontier in Theory

In Michaud MV optimization, there is a difference between the theoretical or limit Michaud MV efficient frontier and the averaging algorithm used in practice to compute it. In the computational procedure, you must decide how many rank portfolios to compute for each equal-return-rank associated simulated MV efficient frontier in Fig. 6.1. The limit of increasing the number of rank portfolios defines the continuous theoretical Michaud efficient frontier. Any point on the theoretical Michaud efficient frontier can be approximated with any desired accuracy simply by increasing the number of computed rank portfolios of simulated MV efficient frontiers. In practical experience, computing a hundred equal-return-rank portfolios may often be sufficient for many applications.[2] At the limit of increased ranks, the theoretically continuous Michaud frontier replaces the continuous Markowitz frontier as an improved definition of portfolio optimality in the MV optimization framework.[3] At each point, the practical approximation and theoretical limit Michaud efficient frontier are the average of properly associated simulated MV optimal portfolios. It is the limit Michaud efficient frontier that should be the focus of theoretical studies of Michaud MV optimization.

Michaud Better Diversification?

We display the portfolio composition map of the Michaud efficient frontier in Fig. 6.4 and compare to Markowitz in Fig. 5.2. Note the dramatic differences between the composition map of optimal portfolios. Notably, while all the securities that were included in the optimization universe in the definition of Michaud portfolio optimality appear in Fig. 6.4, many are excluded in 5.2. Note also the smooth non-linear character of the asset allocations across the spectrum of optimized portfolio risk in 6.4 versus 5.2. The smooth allocation changes across the risk spectrum in Michaud optimization are one of the most important investment and client managerial benefits relative to Markowitz. No additional information is assumed in Michaud relative to Markowitz.[4]

The theoretical and practical implications of Fig. 5.2, relative to 6.4, should not be underestimated. Michaud MV optimization is the consequence of considering risk-return estimate uncertainty in a Markowitz MV efficient frontier framework. Michaud does not overweight the effect of unlikely outlier estimates that can dominate and create instability in Markowitz optimization. The data teach that the extremes as well as all portfolios across the

---

[2] The ERR algorithm is one of a number of algorithms that may be convenient for computing the Michaud frontier. One alternative is arc-length averaging of simulated frontiers that can deal with issues associated with the shape of the frontier and hard to compute points. Interpolation methods can also be used to speed up applications for practice.

[3] The theoretical Michaud frontier is continuous but not differentiable.

[4] It is necessary to note a technical issue that the risk spectrum of standard deviation risk from minimum variance to maximum estimated return of the Michaud MV optimized portfolios in Fig. 6.3 is displayed in terms of ranks from 1 to 100. This is because the ERR was defined to compute 100 return-ranked set of optimized portfolios from Markowitz. Rank order is a more general and convenient framework for direct comparison between Markowitz and Michaud optimized portfolios. Ranks are also consistent with a more realistic understanding of the investment value of MV portfolio optimization in a multivariate statistical estimation context. However, it also indicates that rank 1 or 100 Michaud is not the Markowitz optimized portfolio. The end points of the Michaud frontier start with more risk at the bottom and end with less risk at the top.

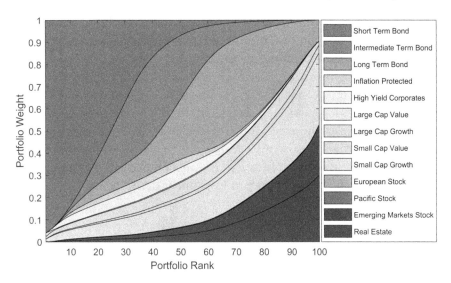

Fig. 6.4 Michaud efficient frontier composition map: Thirteen Vanguard indices 1/2001–12/2020

risk levels of the Michaud frontier are better diversified. One consequence of better diversification is that the Michaud frontier range of optimized risk portfolios does not extend as far on the risk spectrum as Markowitz. While no set of better diversified portfolios can guarantee superior performance relative to Markowitz out-of-sample in any given period, it can provide a more statistically relevant and investment reliable set of investments for risk management in many cases of investment practice.

A Foundation for Portfolio Resampling

In an important recent paper surveying many different issues of portfolio optimization in contemporary finance, Frahm (2015) makes the case that the Michaud resampling procedure can be provided with a theoretical foundation that explains its investment value in practice. This is because "… the Michaud approach aims at eliminating the variance of the investment strategy."[5] Consequently, in the absence of a sufficient level of information, reducing the impact of extreme forecasts as defined by the Michaud procedure is likely the right decision.

In Frahm, the level of information presumed by the investor is crucial for his argument. Consider an analyst with a significant amount of information,

---

[5] Frahm (2015, p. 117).

but not certainty. The investment may be deployed either in a Markowitz or Michaud optimizer. As an operations research optimizer, Markowitz assumes essentially 100 percent certainty in risk-return inputs. But in practice, the Markowitz level of required uncertainty will often be inconsistent with the essential views of the analyst. There is always some level of uncertainty in an investment process in practice. In such cases, the Michaud investor will often benefit from less extreme allocations for portfolios of investment interest.[6] From the perspective of existential reality, where all events have some level of uncertainty, the typical investor is very generally well advised to consider some Michaud frontier uncertainty in investment decisions.[7]

Back Test Limitations

Efforts to prove that a new procedure enhances investment value in modern finance and institutional practice almost always results in the notion of a back test. Such a procedure entails using some set of usually historical return data to show how the given procedure worked relative to another or set of others over the period of study. As is usually the case, the new procedure performs better in the study's test data relative to others and is deemed to be preferable or superior. There are many variations on the back test theme. Some relatively sophisticated approaches "train" the new and test procedure on some data and then test the performance of the procedures on a "hold out" data set. Since the procedures were not trained on the hold out data (which depends on the honesty and reputation of the author), then it may be concluded that the outperformance on a return or risk basis is reliable.

Unfortunately, even the most sophisticated set of procedures cannot claim proof of likely superior outperformance out-of-sample with a back test. This is because, a back test is ultimately an example of how the procedure worked over a particular period of time. There is no guarantee that the procedure would work in any other time period including, most importantly, any future period. Many academic studies of factors in capital markets use sophisticated statistical procedures and often long historical periods of time in an effort to capture the presumed "structural" character of some financial market.[8] But,

---

[6] The issue is that the Markowitz optimized portfolios at the extremes of any given MV efficient frontier are unlikely to be of much investment management interest.

[7] In essence, as a practical matter, Frahm's notion of a "signal" investor does not exist in normal asset management.

[8] It is highly arguable that the presumed "structural" or "stable" economic structure of any financial market is largely an artifact of long-term in-sample statistical estimation. Investment professionals are well aware that equity market structure can change dramatically over investment relevant time

as noted in Chapter 3, sub-periods of poor performance often make such procedures inappropriate for implementation for investment relevant periods irrespective of the length of historical data. Few, if any, back tests can claim reliable out-of-sample investment performance relative to alternatives.[9]

Efficient Frontier Simulation Tests

Michaud (1998, Ch. 6) presented the first rigorously applied multinormal multi-asset Monte Carlo simulation study for estimating the investment enhancement potential of Michaud optimization, relative to Markowitz, for sign and BC MV optimized portfolios. The results showed that, on average, out-of-sample performance was superior for Michaud relative to Markowitz across the risk spectrum of optimized portfolios for the eighteen years of historical returns in the eight asset case data set. This chapter repeats the simulation tests in Michaud (1998) based on thirteen Vanguard indices in Fig. 5.1 for twenty years of monthly returns.[10]

In the simulations, the distribution of the historical twenty-year monthly return vectors is assumed multinormal. In each simulation, the referee hands the Markowitz and Michaud investors twenty years or 240 vectors of monthly multivariate normal simulated returns for the thirteen assets based on the original data. The Michaud and Markowitz investors compute risk-return optimization inputs from the simulated returns, compute the MV efficient frontier portfolios, and hand back the optimized portfolios for the referee to score based on the referee's original data. The simulations are repeated 240 times, consistent with the twenty years of returns in the historical data set. The referee computes the results on average for each of the one hundred return rank Michaud efficient and critical line Markowitz optimized portfolios with the ERR algorithm. The resulting portfolios are shown in Fig. 6.5.[11]

The graphic in Fig. 6.5 shows the in-sample Markowitz and Michaud frontiers and the out-of-sample average performance of the Michaud and

---

periods. Moreover, the highly studied American stock market may often reflect persistent cultural issues inconsistent with other international markets. See Michaud (1999) for some evidence of cultural differences between financial markets.

[9] See Hume (1784) for an authoritative discussion for the limits of knowledge that apply to forecasts.

[10] The description of the in-sample and out-of-sample experiment follows Michaud (1998, Ch. 6) for the Fig. 5.1 data.

[11] The reported simulations of average out-of-sample Markowitz and Michaud optimized portfolios are based on 1000 simulations of the computed MV efficient frontiers using the EER and assuming multinormal distribution.

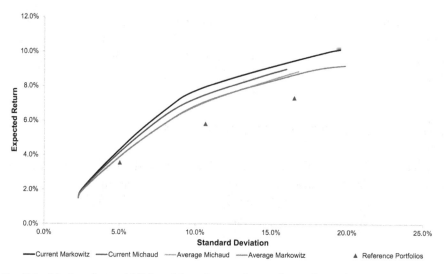

Fig. 6.5 Markowitz and Michaud frontiers and out-of-sample performance: Thirteen Vanguard indices 1/2001–12/2020

Markowitz MV optimized portfolios under the referee's data. The maximum return Markowitz portfolio exhibits slightly more out-of-sample return than Michaud. While not visible, the Markowitz minimum variance port- folios exhibit slightly less out-of-sample risk. Note that the twenty-year average performance of three reference portfolios—equal bonds, 60/40 equal bonds/stocks, equal stocks—plotted in the graphic underperformed both Markowitz and Michaud out-of-sample.

The proper interpretation of the results of Fig. 6.5 goes to the heart of the limitations of any simulation "proof" of investment superiority. In this example, a good deal of information is attributed to the investor in the form of twenty years of monthly IID multinormal returns. This level of infor- mation is very likely far more than any investor in practice could or would assume. Because of the assumed level of information, the simulation is quite certain that the referee's information is correct. What is extremely interesting is that the Michaud investor still does as well from a risk-return basis as Markowitz on average. But there is great uncertainty that the referee's data is correct. It is only one possible realization of the future. Since the referee's view of the future is almost certainly not correct, the Michaud player who assumes uncertainty in information is very much advantaged and very likely the dominant player under almost any other out-of-sample scenario. This is because Michaud in all cases invests with a far better diversified portfolio than Markowitz and is far less dependent than the Markowitz investor that the referee is correct about the future.

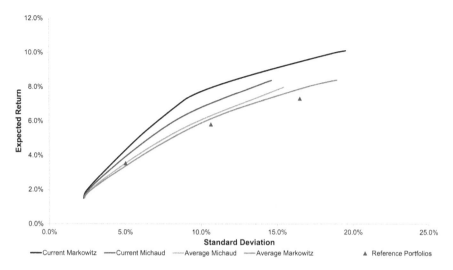

Fig. 6.6 Markowitz and Michaud frontiers and out-of-sample performance: Thirteen Vanguard indices 1/2001–12/2020: 40 monthly return simulations

To help further understand the simulation results in Fig. 6.5, consider the very different referee scenario in Fig. 6.6 based on the same historical data with the different assumption of 40 months of simulated IID multinormal returns. As the panel demonstrates, the results of a Monte Carlo simulation of return are very dependent on the level of information assumed in the referee's risk-return inputs. The out-of-sample results show that the Michaud player is, on average, superior to Markowitz across the span of efficient portfolios. It is also interesting to note that the reference portfolios appear to outperform many Markowitz portfolios. The reliable conclusion is that, under a wide range of possible scenarios, the Michaud player is likely to be superior to Markowitz on average out-of-sample. As Frahm (2015) noted, the level of information assumed in the investment process does have a major impact on the average out-of-sample investment performance of Michaud relative to Markowitz investing.

The Markowitz-Usmen Challenge

Markowitz and Usmen (MU) (2003) tested the Michaud procedure against Markowitz optimization using an enhanced out-of-sample simulation test framework in the case of the Michaud (1998) eight asset class historical data set for three sets of utility functions. In this instance, the comparison includes the use of a Bayesian information enhancement procedure for risk-return esti-mation by the Markowitz investor but not by Michaud. The intent was to show that Markowitz with better (Bayesian estimated) inputs could outper-form Michaud. Unlike Michaud (1998, Ch. 6) or in Fig. 6.6, the Markowitz referee prior spawns ten different simulated priors that lead to 10 simulations for each simulated prior and is all averaged back to the original Markowitz referee prior. The simulation framework introduced by MU is a significantly more sophisticated version of the simulation test in Michaud (1998) where the objective is to remove any significant bias introduced by the referee's prior.

In spite of the Bayesian estimation MU enhancement, the results were not what Markowitz had anticipated. In thirty out of thirty tests, the Michaud procedure proved superior. While there were some details that tended to improve the ratio of failures of the Markowitz procedure, the bottom line indicated a definite win by Michaud optimization. Michaud optimization remains the only algorithm with simulation evidence of on average superior investment effectiveness out-of-sample in a well-defined investment program in the world today.[12]

Different Levels of Investment Information

Journal editors and book publishers generally mandate the use of histor-ical data for evaluating the performance of different investment strategies and optimization algorithms. One important reason is the interest of repro-ducibility of the presented results for interested readers. While the sentiment and objective are well intended, few if any asset managers, tasked at the workbench for managing investment performance, use only historical data in their development of risk-return estimates. Multiple sources of information and procedures are generally used to define risk-return inputs for portfolio management. Consequently, the number of simulations of vectors of returns for simulating optimization inputs in practice is seldom solely a matter of replication of the number of returns in a historical data set.

[12] Markowitz and Usmen (2003) remain the only published test of Michaud versus Markowitz at this writing that is free of errors of procedure and interpretation. Comments on errors in prior experiments are available on www.researchgate.com, www.ssrn.com and www.newfrontieradvisors.com.

Investment Uncertainty

The number of simulated return vectors from a multivariate normal statistical distribution to compute risk-return estimates is a fundamental parameter of the Michaud efficient frontier procedure. It is the method for converting Markowitz portfolio optimization into linear constrained multinormal least squares linear regression. Figure 6.7 illustrates this effect. As the number of the average of simulations of multinormal vector returns increases, the Michaud frontier approaches similarity to the referee's in-sample data and the Markowitz solution. Conversely, as the number of the average of simulations of vector returns decreases, the Michaud frontier approaches equal or benchmark index weighting. In the first case, Michaud approaches perfect certainty relative to the referee's data, in the second the no-information prior.

In Michaud optimization, the essential nature of Michaud MV optimization is that of a procedure for including the assumed amount of confidence or level of uncertainty in the investor's information in the optimization for defining portfolio optimality. It is worth noting that simulating ten years of IID multinormal distributed vectors of monthly returns may often represent far more information than any available in a comparable historical data set of monthly returns or in a manager's risk-return estimates.

In practice, how to set the number of vector return simulations for replicating the intuitive notion of investor information uncertainty for a set of

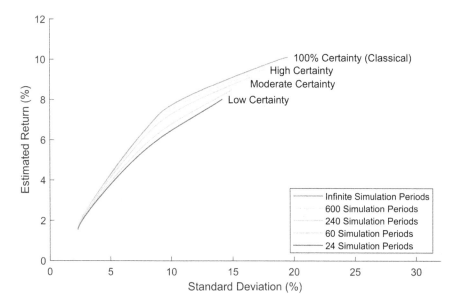

Fig. 6.7 Confidence level efficient frontiers

risk-return estimates is a matter of investment manager expertise. To facilitate use in practice, it may be useful to use a logarithmic scale for setting the number of simulations of vector returns, with an index from 1 to 10, to implement the intuitive notion of relative levels of uncertainty. However, any scale may require customization for a given asset management strategy or institution.

The Necessity of the Forecast Uncertainty Parameter

While the need to set a forecast certainty parameter to properly use Michaud optimization may seem odd or a nuisance at first, upon reflection, having the option should seem far more preferable to any asset manager than having to assume in hindsight the absurd level of investment information certainty typically required for investment useful Markowitz optimization. Not having an option for implementing information uncertainty represents one of the most serious flaws of the Markowitz procedure for practical application.

The interesting question is not whether the forecast certainty parameter is essential but rather how best to set it. The certainty level of a market strategist's outlook is likely to vary over time. An investment manager may want to reflect a client's uncertainty in the portfolios they design. A manager's style for asset management will often impact the level of certainty. For example, a value manager may have less short-term certainty about the market while a growth stock manager may want to take more aggressive positions. The level of certainty associated with long-term investing may impact how the current portfolio should be optimized. In these cases, and many others, forecast certainty can be seen as an integral part of the process of providing effective MV optimized portfolios.

Can Michaud Optimization Fail

Our simulation experiments do not settle the debate that Michaud optimization is generally preferable to Markowitz. Michaud optimization will often fail as a useful procedure for defining an investment useful diversified investment process when Markowitz also results in a poorly diversified efficient portfolio for some given set of inputs and optimization universe. As Michaud and Esch (2017) explain, for a given case of ten assets in an optimization universe, if some have negative estimated returns, Markowitz optimization is not likely to provide a useful sense of a well-diversified portfolio, and neither will Michaud.[13] The fundamental assumption for the success of any optimization procedure is a well-defined investment program. Otherwise, both Markowitz and Michaud are likely to fail the objective of computing a well-diversified portfolio suitable for funding.

A Distribution-Free Mean–Variance Efficient Frontier

Michaud optimization uses Monte Carlo multivariate normal return simulation of investor estimates of asset risk and return and a U.S. patented investor appropriate averaging of Markowitz frontiers to compute average-return-ranked optimal portfolios. The multivariate normal return distribution is uniquely consistent with Markowitz MV theory parametrization of a quadratic function approximation of investor utility.[14] The ERR algorithm Michaud efficient frontier portfolios form an interval scale of returns, conditional on the level of information associated with the number of simulations of return of Markowitz efficient frontiers.[15]

In the procedure we describe, portfolio optimality is a distribution-free statistical estimate of Markowitz portfolio optimality. There is no presumption of the return distribution of the risk-return parameters that drive the computation. Distribution-free statistical methods may often have fundamentally different statistical characteristics from classical Markowitz efficiency. Scheffé (1943) describes the characteristics and promise of distribution-free statistical estimation[16]:

> The theory of traditional statistical estimation deals with the problem of estimating values of the unknown parameters of distribution functions of specified form from random samples assumed to have been drawn from such populations. This can be referred as the parametric case. Under it falls all the theory based on normality assumptions. Only a very small fraction of the extensive literature of mathematical statistics is devoted to the nonparametric

---

[13] The concept of MV optimized long-short investing when negative returns are important needs to consider a different set of issues as discussed in Michaud (1993).

[14] In Markowitz theory, the portfolios on the MV efficient frontier are presumed good quadratic utility function approximations of investor expected utility.

[15] Investor assumed certainty level of information in risk-return inputs is defined by the number of simulated returns when computing Markowitz frontiers.

[16] The terms "distribution-free" and "nonparametric" are often used interchangeably. See further Kendall and Sundrum (1953) and Wilks (1947).

case, and most has been very recent. The prospects of a theory freed from specific assumptions about the form of the probability distribution should excite both the theoretician and the practitioner, since such a theory might combine elegance of structure with wide applicability.

The Michaud frontier is a distribution-free or nonparametric definition of portfolio optimality.[17] Markowitz optimization as defined is based solely on mean–variance parameters that uniquely define a multivariate normal distribution. The optimization is unconcerned by non-normality or other characteristics of estimated risk-returns. A distribution-free description of portfolio optimality and asset management is potentially more robust and may provide more useful optimized portfolios in practice.[18]

Expected Utility and the Michaud Efficient Frontier

For most of the second half of the twentieth century, modern neoclassical finance, and more generally much of social science, has been based on the VM game theory expected utility axioms as a prescription for rational decision making under uncertainty.[19] Traditional criticism of the Markowitz MV efficient frontier holds that it is inconsistent with VM expected utility maximization except under the unrealistic conditions of an exact normal return distribution or quadratic expected utility function.

Markowitz addressed the issue of the consistency of the Markowitz efficient frontier with investor expected utility estimation in Levy and Markowitz (LM) (1979) and Kroll et al. (KLM) (1984). They argue that portfolios on the Markowitz efficient frontier provide useful and convenient approximations to portfolios that maximize investor expected utility. In the proposed two-step estimation process, compute the Markowitz MV efficient frontier for an investor's estimates of risk and return and then find the portfolio on the Markowitz frontier that maximizes a MV approximation of the investor's

---

[17] The terms nonparametric and distribution-free statistical methodologies generally based on ranks and other order statistics are often used interchangeably though there are some subtle differences as discussed in Kendall and Sundrum (1953) that will not be of concern here.

[18] While it was initially believed that non-parametric methods would often be deficient in robustness compared to more traditional parametric methods, it has become understood that such procedures can have significant advantages relative to their parametric counterparts in terms of efficiency and validity particularly if the assumptions of normality are not well satisfied, as is often the case with financial data.

[19] For example, Fennema and Bezembinder (1995).

expected utility function.[20] The Markowitz LM and KLM framework is proposed to provide convenient approximations to portfolios that maximize investor expected utility for portfolios on the Markowitz MV frontier.

It is, however, of interest to consider the current state of expected utility theory in the context of MV efficient frontiers. As discussed in Chapter 4, Allais (1953) and Tversky and Kahneman (1979, 1992) argue convincingly among many others that human decision making under uncertainty is inconsistent with VM game theory utility axioms. Quiggin (1982, 1993) proposed the rank-dependent expected utility (RDEU) algorithm as a rational expected utility framework that resolves the issues of transitivity and stochastic dominance that arose in the KT framework. Quiggin observes: "The solution is to arrange the states of the world so that the outcomes they yield are ordered from worst to best, then to give each state a weight that depends on its ranking as well its probability."[21] The Quiggin RDEU expected utility theory is the basis of Tversky and Kahneman (1992) cumulative prospect theory, often considered the state of the art of expected utility theory. RDEU theory is not consistent with Markowitz two-step expected utility approximation.

To describe a relationship between Michaud optimization and RDEU expected utility theory, we need to further discuss some properties of the Michaud optimization algorithm. The necessary step in RDEU utility theory is to convert the probability distribution of outcomes into rank ordered from worst to best. This is precisely the function of the Michaud ERR computational algorithm. The procedure converts the assumed investor portfolio risk-return distribution into an interval scale estimated return ranking of MV optimized portfolios. In applications, a probability transformation function can be imposed on the ranks expressing various investor utility characteristics. A linear or concave increasing function is an example that may express increasing risk aversion as a function of increasing ranks. Unlike Markowitz two-step estimation, the Michaud algorithm is no approximation but exactly consistent with the RDEU expected utility framework.

In a well-defined investment program, Michaud optimization will generally provide monotone increasing expected return-ranked optimized portfolios. In this case, the simplest probability weighting function is no weighting at all reflecting investor increasing risk aversion. More generally, RDEU theory allows many alternative frameworks for expected utility estimation with probability transformation functions. The S-shaped function associated with KT can be used to overweight extreme low probability events

---

[20] A linear mean–variance approximation to continuous functions in engineering and many scientific applications is a widely used tool in practice.

[21] Quiggin (1993, p. 63).

and underweight moderate events. A natural investment strategy framework for the S-shaped function is a two-portfolio long-short investment strategy as described in Michaud (1993). While a concave transformation function expressing increasing risk aversion is typically associated with Markowitz frontiers, it may be of interest to consider the implications of a convex transformation function in the context of lotteries and gambles. Clearly, there are many possible examples beyond these simple cases that could be of interest. It is interesting to speculate that many heretofore unexplored investment strategies may also be defined with alternative transformation functions all leading to expected utility consistent strategies.

It is important to note that there is an additional fundamental mismatch between the Quiggin RDEU framework and the estimate uncertainty conditional Michaud efficient frontier. This is the issue of objective probabilities (roulette lotteries) versus subjective probabilities (horse lotteries). To connect RDEU theory to probability estimate uncertainty implicit in Michaud MV optimization requires the Choquet (1953–1954) integral. In this context, probabilities need to be replaced with a σ-field of subsets of some space Ω where the subsets have the same behavior as utility functions on probabilities.[22] As Wakker (1990) notes, assuming stochastic dominance, RDEU theory with uncertain probabilities is the same as in the certainty case beyond interpretation. No fundamental change in application of RDEU theory to Michaud optimization is required.

Rationality properties should be a minimal condition for the definition of a valuable and effective investment strategy. RDEU expected utility consistent MV optimization provides a rich convenient framework for reliable and investment meaningful asset management in practice that did not exist before. The investor convenient Markowitz optimization framework, in the context of the Michaud generalization, provides a valuable theoretical basis that should reassure investors and theoreticians alike.

Markowitz 2005 Efficient Frontier Triangle

It is of interest to note that theoretically the Michaud MV efficient frontier is contained within the Markowitz (2005) MV efficient frontier triangle discussed at the end of Chapter 5. How deep within the triangle depends on the level of confidence of information in the risk-return estimates. Many standard market indices may reside within the Michaud efficient frontier region

---

[22] See the discussion in Quiggin (1993, sec. 5.7).

that is contained within the Markowitz triangle. Our results do not invalidate the Markowitz proposition that the theoretical CAPM "market" portfolio is unlikely MV efficient or very useful for defining MV portfolio optimality in the traditional institutional framework of index-relative MV optimization.

Michaud Is not Markowitz

The result of a Michaud optimization is conventionally displayed as a MV efficient frontier comparable to Markowitz. However, the essential nature of the procedure is as an average of properly ERR associated Markowitz MV optimal portfolios in N-dimensional risk-return portfolio space. As in any statistical estimation procedure, Michaud optimization can be misused; the data have to make sense for the purpose of the application. It is often the case that the Michaud efficient frontier will not mirror the concave character of Markowitz and will not have an increasing concave relationship of expected return relative to portfolio standard deviation or ranks. But it is not necessary that the Michaud frontier has the shape of an iconic concave curve Markowitz frontier as claimed in Scherer (2002). As explained in Michaud and Michaud (2008a, pp. 53–54), the Michaud frontier may have a max estimated return optimized portfolio point where all optimized portfolios with higher levels of risk are not Michaud MV efficient. In addition, it is incorrect to claim that a scalloping or non-concave section of the frontier implies that more efficient portfolios can be found on a linear segment than those on the frontier.[23]

MV optimization in practice is most appropriate for experienced investment professionals in the context of a well-defined investment program.[24] As multivariate statistical estimation, Michaud optimization is subject to the well-known limitations of badly defined statistical practice familiar in authoritative teachings in multivariate linear regression studies and applications. A necessary condition for a well-defined Michaud MV portfolio optimization is a set of assets and risk-return estimates that are considered to provide significant diversification benefit across the spectrum of portfolios on the efficient frontier. The appropriateness of any data set in a multivariate statistical estimation procedure is widely understood as a necessary presumption for the success of any statistical estimation. Michaud optimization requires

---

[23] Also claimed in Scherer (2002).

[24] Weiner (1964) provides an iconic description of the issue for computer science algorithms.

such an appropriate set of risk-return estimates to facilitate construction of a well-defined Investment program.[25]

Summary

The Michaud efficient frontier represents a linear constrained MV parameter-based expected utility framework consistent with Quiggin (1982, 1993) RDEU theory of equal return interval scale rankings of MV optimized portfolios.[26] Multinormal simulation experiments demonstrate the likely on average out-of-sample superiority of Michaud optimized portfolio perfor-mance relative to Markowitz for well-defined investment programs.[27] Michaud optimization solves the instability and ambiguity of Markowitz optimality with estimation error sensitive technology. The concept of ranked optimality rather than risk-return maximization redefines the meaning of Markowitz MV optimization in a more realistic investment framework. The integrity of a unique and rigorous expected utility framework for asset management in an investor convenient Markowitz MV framework should comfort thoughtful investors and finance theoreticians alike. Experienced investors often find Michaud optimality investment intuitive and practical without the need of many ad hoc constraints. The consequence is likely more robust and relevant portfolio performance relative to objectives.

References

Allais, M. 1953. Le comportement de l'homme rationnel devant le risque: Critique des postulats et axioms de l'école Americaine. *Econometrica* 21 (4): 503–546.

Choquet, G. 1953–1954. Theory of Capacities. *Annales Institut Fourier* 5: 131–295.

Fennema, H., and T. Bezembinder. 1995. Book Review: J. Quiggin, 'Generalized Expected Utility: The Rank Dependent Model.' *Acta Psychologica* 88: 79–81.

Frahm, G. 2015. A Theoretical Foundation of Portfolio Resampling. *Theory and Decision* 79 (1): 107–132.

Hume, D. 1784. *Philosophical Essays Concerning Human Understanding*. London.

Kahneman, D., and A. Tversky. 1979. Prospect Theory: An Analysis of Decision Under Risk. *Econometrica* 47 (2): 263–291.

---

[25] One simple method is to run a Markowitz optimization that excludes many assets in the optimized portfolios.

[26] The equal return rank averaging procedure may not always be most appropriate for meeting objectives.

[27] Michaud (1998, Ch.6), Markowitz and Usmen (2003), and Michaud and Michaud (2008a, b).

Kendall, M.G., and R.M. Sundrum. 1953. Distribution-Free Methods and Order Properties. *Review of the International Statistical Institute* 3: 124–134.

Kroll, Y., H. Levy, and H. Markowitz. 1984. Mean-Variance Versus Direct Utility Maximization. *Journal of Finance* 39 (1): 47–61.

Levy, H., and H. Markowitz. 1979. Approximating Expected Utility by a Function of the Mean and the Variance. *American Economic Review* 69 (3): 308–317.

Markowitz, H. 1952. Portfolio Selection. *Journal of Finance* 7 (1): 77–91.

Markowitz, H. 2005. Market Efficiency: A Theoretical Distinction and So What? *Financial Analysts Journal* 61 (5): 17–30.

Markowitz, H., and N. Usmen. 2003. Resampled Frontiers Versus Diffuse Bayes: An Experiment. *Journal of Investment Management* 1 (4): 9–25.

Michaud, R. 1993. Are Long-Short Equity Strategies Superior? *Financial Analyst Journal* 49 (6): 44–49.

Michaud, R. 1998. *Efficient Asset Management: A Practical Guide to Stock Portfolio Optimization and Asset Allocation.* Boston: Harvard Business School Press.

Michaud, R. 1999. *Investment Styles, Market Anomalies, and Global Stock Selection.* Charlottesville: Research Foundation of the Chartered Financial Institute.

Michaud, R., and D. Esch. 2017. When Michaud Optimization Fails. Available at: https://newfrontieradvisors.com/media/1488/mofjan2018.pdf

Michaud, R., and R. Michaud. 2008a. *Efficient Asset Management: A Practical Guide to Stock Portfolio Optimization and Asset Allocation.* New York: Oxford University Press. 1st ed. 1998, originally published by Harvard Business School Press, Boston.

Michaud, R., and R. Michaud. 2008b. Estimation Error and Portfolio Optimization: A Resampling Solution. *Journal of Investment Management* 6 (1): 8–28.

Quiggin, J. 1982. A Theory of Anticipated Utility. *Journal of Economic Behavior and Organization* 3 (4): 323–343.

Quiggin, J. 1993. *Generalized Expected Utility Theory: The Rank-Dependent Model.* London: Kluwer Academic Publishers.

Scheffé, H. 1943. Statistical Inference in the Non-parametric Case. *The Annals of Mathematical Statistics* 14: 305–332.

Scherer, B. 2002. Portfolio Resampling: Review and Critique. *Financial Analysts Journal* 58 (6): 98–109.

Tversky, A., and D. Kahneman. 1992. Advances in Prospect Theory: Cumulative representation of Uncertainty. *Journal of Risk and Uncertainty* 5: 297–323.

Wakker, P. 1990. Under stochastic dominance Choquet - expected utility and anticipated utility are identical. *Theory and Decision* 29: 119–132.

Weiner, N. 1964. Intellectual Honesty and the Contemporary Scientist. *Technology Review* 1718 (April): 45–47.

Wilks, S.S. 1947. Order Statistics. Address Delivered Before the Summer Meeting of the Society in New Haven by invitation of the Committee to Select Hour Speakers for Annual and Summer Meetings.

7

An Enhanced Investment Process

Successful asset management requires not only construction of investment effective portfolios but also an investment process of continuous monitoring and efficient trading over time. Portfolios necessarily age and drift from optimal weights. Clients often need to revise investment objectives relative to changes in markets and lifestyles. But current rebalancing methods and trading rules are typically ad hoc and likely suboptimal. This chapter proposes defining using the machinery of Monte Carlo simulation to define novel techniques to address a critical range of essential investment management functions. The results lead to new statistical estimation methods for solving standard portfolio management issues not available with traditional methods.

Portfolio Rebalancing in Practice

Portfolio rebalancing in institutional and retail investor practice is often calendar based. Managers may rebalance a portfolio on a once a month, once a quarter, once a year, every day, or just before the client comes to visit. In calendar-based rebalancing, the portfolio is routinely checked for optimality and trades recommended on a fixed schedule similar to the advice professional mechanics recommend on servicing a car every six months. But such a procedure is clearly suboptimal. It ignores times between the calendar schedule when rebalancing may have been advisable or trading in noise.

Market volatility varies in time, and the impact of suboptimality of a fixed schedule can be cumulatively significant over time.

A second popular rebalancing decision rule is to establish a "normal" range of variation in portfolio weights for every security in the portfolio. If the weight of an asset drifts outside its normal range in some time period, the portfolio is said to need rebalancing because it is no longer "optimal." The procedure is far from an optimal trading rule in two important ways. The definition of normal ranges for each asset is ad hoc. There is no theory to define the procedure. Also the procedure is asset, not portfolio, based. As a result, the overall risk and optimality of the portfolio itself are ignored. This is often a serious issue since the "overweight" of one or several assets may be compensated for by an "underweight" for some assets or set of assets that leave the overall risk of the portfolio stable. The procedure may often require more frequent rebalancing and trading than may be optimal.

Quantitative equity portfolio managers may rebalance a portfolio depending on the size of estimated portfolio alpha relative to the cost of trading. When alpha is greater, trade; if less, trading may not be warranted. The usefulness of the procedure requires a realistic estimate of portfolio alpha and trading cost. But the alpha forecast is an estimate reflecting an aspirational or orange dollar scale, while trading cost estimates are designed to reflect a more substantive though variable and still uncertain green dollar scale. It is unlikely that the relative size of the two estimates has consistent usefulness for deciding when to trade.

Portfolio Statistical Similarity

The correct framework for deciding when to trade is whether the current portfolio is statistically similar to, or distinct from, the currently estimated optimal portfolio. If two portfolios are statistically similar, trading is not warranted. The result would be likely trading in noise. If the two portfolios are statistically dissimilar, trading may be warranted. Unlike traditional methods, the decision to rebalance and trade is portfolio based and independent of time, ad hoc ranges, and scale of alpha. The decision depends solely on the statistical nature of the two portfolios at any given point in time.

It has been understood since Shanken (1986) and Jobson and Korkie (1986) that the correct definition of a portfolio rebalancing rule should be statistical similarity between owned and current optimal portfolios. But the academic procedures are not useful for asset management in practice. This is because the statistical procedures are available only for BC MV optimized portfolios. Investment portfolios are inequality constrained making the academic procedures invalid and highly misleading for practice.

A Practical Portfolio Similarity Test

The first practical statistical similarity test between optimized and candidate linear constrained portfolios was given in Michaud (1998, Ch. 7). The procedure uses multinormal resampling technology to compute a need-to-trade probability between two given linear constrained portfolios. The procedure is a distribution-free algorithm that is an application of Michaud optimization technology.

As indicated in Chapter 5, each point on the Michaud efficient frontier is an average of properly associated simulated MV optimized portfolios. Compute the relative variance of each of the properly associated simulated MV optimal portfolios sorted from smallest to largest for a given optimized portfolio.[1] The sorted variances provide a measure of the normal range of distances of portfolios in N-dimensional portfolio space. Now compute the relative variance of the current portfolio from computed optimal. The percent of portfolios in the sort of relative variance distance measures can be found. If only 10% of the portfolios that make up the averaging process for defining an optimal point on the Michaud frontier are closer, trading may not seem advisable. The candidate seems functionally close to optimal. However, if 90% of the portfolios associated with the optimal portfolio are closer, trading may be advisable.

The procedure is illustrated in Fig. 6.2 for simulated 60/40 Markowitz MV optimized portfolios. As can be observed, the statistical test area is highly unstable both above and below the 60/40 point for the Vanguard thirteen index fund securities. Intuitively, the test area does not seem very well conditioned for an unbiased statistical test.

Similarity Test Enhancements

The original Michaud portfolio rebalancing rule has gone through a number of important iterations since described in Michaud (1998, Ch. 7) illustrated for the thirteen Vanguard indices data in Fig. 7.1. In the original rule, the MV

---

[1] Alternative norms could be used but relative variance measures distance in N-dimensional portfolio space and likely most appropriate for professional asset management.

associated simulated portfolios were Markowitz optimized. Meta-resampled simulations methods, first proposed by Robert Michaud and described in Michaud and Michaud (2002), have been introduced to replace association of (parent) simulated Markowitz optimal portfolios in the distance function with associated (child) simulated Michaud optimized portfolios.

A second major refinement of the procedure had to do with the problem of overlapping data. Suppose six months of drift of an optimized portfolio. A new optimal portfolio may be based on much similar information in its construction from the original optimized portfolio. For example, many equity risk models result from regressions based on five years of monthly data. So six months later, the new optimal portfolio and the owned portfolio will have four and a half years of common risk model data. All other things the same, the new portfolio may often seem statistically similar according to the procedure. Michaud et al. (2012) describe a new procedure where meta-resampled efficient frontiers used to compute the new Michaud efficient frontier portfolios are based only on data available in the non-overlapping time period. The non-overlapping rebalancing rule algorithm is further described in Exhibit 7.1.

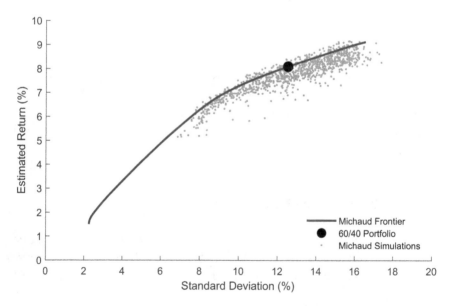

Fig. 7.1 Meta-resampled statistical rebalancing 60/40 Michaud optimized; 12 months trade horizon

Exhibit 7.1 Non-overlapping Rebalancing Rule Algorithm

Consider one year ago computed optimal portfolio P_0.

> Let $X_0 = [x_1, x_2, \ldots x_{60}]$ original 60 months risk-return distribution.
> Compute the new optimal portfolio P^* with 60 months of data including new 6 months data.
> Let $X_{new} = [x_7, x_8, \ldots x_{66}] =$ defines new risk-return distribution.
> Note 48 months of common information: $[x_7, x_8, \ldots x_{66}]$.
> Compute meta-resampled portfolios (simplest case)
>
> > Compute k = random draws = 6 from X_{new} distribution
> > Add to common 54 months: $[x_7, x_8, \ldots x_{66}]$ to compute new simulated optimal portfolio.
> > Compute meta-sim optimal and distance to P^*
> > Repeat above many times
>
> Sort and define distance distribution
> Compute P_0 distance to optimal.
> Percentile in distance distribution = conditional need-to-trade probability

In this new procedure, illustrated in Fig. 7.1, properly associated meta-resampled Michaud optimized portfolios are used in defining the relative variance in the sorting computation. The results include the assumption of twenty years of Monte Carlo resampled risk returns to compute the Michaud Frontier and one year of simulated monthly "new" returns for the overlapping data rebalancing procedure. There are 1000 simulated Michaud-Esch associated MV optimal portfolios displayed in the graphic.

As can be observed when comparing Fig. 7.1 to 6.2, the statistical area for the new test is far less tilted above or below the 60/40 optimal portfolio on the Michaud frontier. There is also a reduced size of the N-dimensional "football" that tends to enhance the investment significance of the no-need-to-trade rule. The new procedure results in substantially more statistical power across the spectrum of efficient frontier risk. These and other refinements including a number of computational efficiencies provide an investment useful portfolio monitoring decision rule that has been in actual investment practice for more than ten years.

What we have described is a nonparametric statistical distribution-based stopping rule for portfolio rebalancing. While a manager does not want to trade in noise, trading when effective is very desirable. The procedure provides a simple reasonably investment intuitive rule to consider whether to trade. If the need-to-trade probability is consistently greater than 50% over some relevant time period, trading will often seem justifiable. In practice, the rule has often avoided trading even when more traditional methods were flashing trade. However, any decision rule for trading should be customized to the characteristics of information available, investor or institution objectives, investment style, and many other issues.[2]

Note on Simulation Research

It has probably not escaped the notice of readers that the procedures described for defining optimized portfolios in the prior chapter and rebalancing rules above may often require highly compute intensive procedures. In the Michaud et al. (2002) enhancement of the trading probability estimate, each simulated Markowitz portfolio requires the computation of a Michaud efficient frontier which in itself requires multiple computations of simulated efficient frontiers. A straightforward computation of 100 Markowitz frontiers requires 100 times one hundred meta-resampled frontier computations. Many of the procedures currently used in Michaud optimization and Michaud-Esch rebalancing would not have been commercially viable in the not very distant past. Some of the experiments for prototype testing, defining, developing, and refining have often taken many hours or even days of computation even with the fastest desktops and laptops then available.

But refinements can reduce the amount of clock time required to compute the procedures when implemented. Dr. David Esch has implemented a table lookup procedure for accessing relative variance computations for a given set of portfolios on the Michaud frontier that can substantially reduce the clock time to compute rebalancing probabilities in applications. Nevertheless, Monte Carlo statistical simulation procedures will often require far more computation time than familiar traditional tools in asset management. This should not be seen as a limitation. Modern statistical techniques in actual practice in many scientific fields depend on highly compute intense Monte Carlo simulation methods. Procedures at the frontiers of science in many fields may take hours, days or even weeks of computation even with the fastest of available computers. If you are trying to solve real problems, it is no great limitation to use compute intensive methods. In the cases presented here, this is just finance catching up to the statistical sophistication of other scientific fields.

---

[2] See Michaud et al. (2012) for further discussion on customizing the rebalancing rule.

A Note on Optimization and Multivariate Linear Regression

In the familiar budget-constrained only case, where the mean of the dependent variable is subtracted from the data in the linear regression, the minimum variance Markowitz MV optimized portfolio is the same as the multivariate normal least squares linear regression. In fact, the author's original objective in Michaud (1998) was to find a way to solve Markowitz instability and ambiguity by estimating the statistical variance of the allocations in the optimized portfolio as in standard multivariate linear regression analysis. But inequality constraints on asset weights requires quadratic programming methods and is not possible to solve as a conventional multivariate linear regression. However, it is often useful as a heuristic to think of Markowitz and Michaud MV optimization as a special form of constrained multivariate linear regression.

Various probability distributions, such as the multivariate t-distribution, may be useful in defining the ERR algorithm resampling process in applications. In general, Michaud optimization represents a new class of distribution-free multivariate linear regression that may have applications for other linear constrained multivariate estimation applications beyond MV portfolio optimization.

Simulation and Optimized Portfolio Analysis

Distribution-free statistical simulation methods may have surprising power to analyze the character of a MV optimization. For example, a portfolio manager may have great interest in deciding the importance of a particular security or set of securities in an optimized portfolio. Some assets may have a dominant role while others may not be simulation important or significant.

Figure 7.2 illustrates this important technique for understanding the role of an asset across the spectrum of optimized portfolio risk. In this case, we consider two Vanguard index funds in the thirteen Vanguard optimization case in Fig. 5.1: intermediate government bonds and small cap stocks. The left-hand side of Fig. 7.2 describes the 25th and 75th percentile ranges and Michaud optimized asset allocation weights of the Small Cap Growth Stock index in the Michaud efficient frontier across the 100 ranks of optimized portfolios. Similarly, the right-hand side describes the data for the 25th and 75th percentiles and Michaud optimized asset allocation weights of the small cap growth equity index across the one hundred ranks of optimized portfolios. In the small cap growth stock case, the allocations are more prominent at the high end of the efficient frontier while in the intermediate bond case, the allocations are more prominent in the middle of the efficient frontier. The trade horizon is set to twelve months of non-overlapping simulated monthly returns.

The analyses illustrated here are available for any asset in the optimization universe. The procedure is very flexible; for example, the ranges of the allocations can be set to 10/90% or 5/95% at the analyst's option. While comparisons relative to other assets are often of interest, the analyses for any individual asset have its own set of information for understanding its role in adding optimality and diversification in the optimized portfolio.

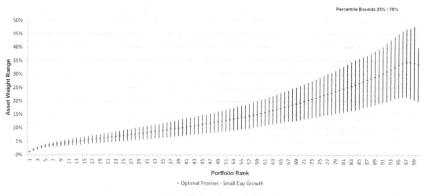

Small Cap Growth Stocks

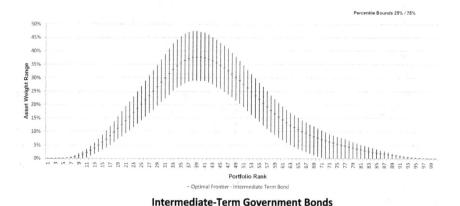

Intermediate-Term Government Bonds

Fig. 7.2 Security simulation significance analysis: 240 month Michaud-Esch return simulations, 12 months trade horizon

These kinds of analyses are uniquely available in a simulation framework for signed constrained MV optimization where the trade horizon is part of the meta-resampled simulation procedure.

Trade Advisor

Once a decision has been made that a portfolio is statistically suboptimal and requires trading, the next consideration is how to trade efficiently. While it is always possible to completely revise the original portfolio by replacing it with its new optimal, such a procedure is very generally trading cost inefficient. It is also not a common practice. Managers typically tend to identify key assets that require trading while possibly leaving much of the remaining portfolio unchanged.

A "trade advisor" panel, first proposed by Robert Michaud and refined by David Esch, provides a framework for defining a statistically cost-efficient trade of the current portfolio relative to Michaud efficient target. The conceptual key for defining statistical trade efficiency is given in Fig. 7.3 below.

The horizontal axis in Fig. 7.3 defines the turnover level of the convex sum parameter of the current relative to target portfolio from zero on the left-hand side to 100% on the right-hand side. The trade path of two portfolios, Port a and Port b, are also displayed; both begin at 100% need-to-trade probability at the top left-hand side to zero at the bottom right-hand side as a function of turnover. The figure shows that, for portfolio a, the need-to-trade probability declines quickly relative to portfolio b as a function of turnover of the convex sum portfolio. The right-hand side axis identifies a point of desired "similarity level" of statistical equivalence relative to target in terms of the need-to-trade probability. The intersection of the similarity level for Port a indicates far less turnover required for trading at the given similarity level than is the case for Port b.

What we have presented in Fig. 7.3 is a "stopping rule" for efficient trading that is enabled with the device of the Michaud-Esch need-to-trade probability estimate. For either Portfolio a or Portfolio b, the statistically efficient rule requires far less trading than completely trading to target. The great benefit of the trade advisor procedure relative to traditional practice is that the statistical rule replaces ad hoc methods widely in place in practice. A rigorous rule is unlikely to be conservative when required but ineffective when necessary.

In practice, if the current portfolio was not a Michaud optimized portfolio, the need-to-trade probability may often indicate nearly wholesale revision to

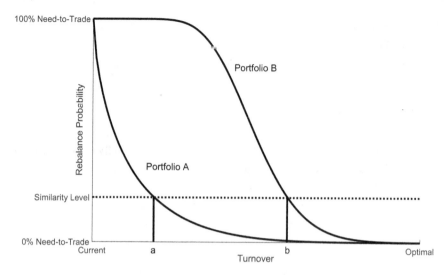

Fig. 7.3 Statistical trade-efficiency framework

target. On the other hand, for a current Michaud optimized portfolio, the rule may indicate relatively limited trading for optimality similarity all other things the same. Of course, such considerations also depend on investment objectives, investor horizon, investment styles, and other issues associated with the desire to trade for a particular case and objectives.

Enhancements

Our discussion of the trade advisor procedure was designed for clarity. The notion that a convex sum of target relative to current portfolio as the natural definition of turnover was used for simplicity. However, in practice, there may be alternatives more convenient or efficient for defining turnover. In specific cases, some assets are more important than others for defining efficient trading. Such discussion is beyond the scope of the text.

Implications for Asset Management

We are in a position to address some of the transcendent questions raised in the Preface of the text: Why does professional active management often underperform standard market indices on a cost-adjusted risk-adjusted basis over relevant investment horizons? Is market informational efficiency the only or even the most likely rationale? The arguments in this and the previous two chapters demonstrate that institutional quantitative asset management has been influenced by likely ineffective theory and ad hoc procedures for more than sixty years. A simple and more productive rationale for resolving persistent active management underperformance is enhanced theory and technology.

We have endeavored to present a unified framework for redefining the investment management process on rigorous modern statistical principles and novel procedures. While asset management has always been fundamentally statistical estimation, what has been unavailable are practical and computationally efficient statistical tools for implementation that address the limitations traditional methods encounter with linear inequality-constrained portfolios. As we have shown, the major components of the investment management process can be implemented with new yet accessible convenient statistical techniques.

References

Michaud, R. 1998. *Efficient Asset Management: A Practical Guide to Stock Portfolio Optimization and Asset Allocation.* Boston: Harvard Business School Press.

Michaud, R., and R. Michaud 2002. Resampled Portfolio Rebalancing and Monitoring. *New Frontier Advisors Newsletter* (4th quarter).

Michaud, R., D. Esch, and R. Michaud. 2012. Portfolio Monitoring in Theory and Practice. *Journal of Investment Management* 10 (4): 5–18.

8

A New Foundation for Financial Markets and Social Science

In the mid-1960s, finance took a critical wrong turn that fundamentally affected the value of theory and the investment effectiveness of quantitative tools for asset management. This was unfortunate since a more reliable foundation had been proposed by Markowitz (1952) and developed in Markowitz (1959). In addition, neoclassical finance, the dominant theory of modern finance for more than sixty years, was also based on expected utility axioms now understood as a flawed investor decision-making framework with major negative consequences for much of investment technology in current practice. We propose to reboot theory by backing up finance to some of the evergreen principles and insights from the early pioneers of twentieth-century finance and social science. We propose a fundamentally different stock market framework based on sociological principles of multiperiod interactions of limited-information rational agents.[1] Equity markets emerge as a central financial intermediary that uniquely facilitates time-transfer savings for meeting long-term investor objectives. The rules governing behavior are not expected utility maxims of individual behavior but rational cognition of best interest sociological norms resulting from interactions among people and their environment that have evolved over time. An alternative perspective emerges of much of preference theory rationalizable from simple efficient patterns of economic behavior.

---

[1] Lo (2004) presents a response to failures of CAPM and EMH theory with a proposal based on a framework of biological adaptation of agents. In contrast, our proposal uses a sociological and psychological framework to address similar issues.

© The Author(s), under exclusive license to Springer Nature Switzerland AG 2023
R. O. Michaud, *Finance's Wrong Turns*,
https://doi.org/10.1007/978-3-031-21863-7_8

Knight Uncertainty

Our journey to define a more useful and realistic path for financial theory and practice begins a hundred years ago with Frank Knight's (1921) classic discussion of information uncertainty in games and financial markets. Knight distinguishes three levels of investment uncertainty:

(1) Winning a random repeatable game.

A roulette wheel in a casino is a simple iconic example of a random repeatable game. In any play of the game, the outcome and value of a gamble are unknown. However, the probability of the casino winning over many plays of the game is stable, known, and positive. The roulette game follows the classical laws of probability theory.

(2) A statistically estimated repeatable event.

Consider estimation of the cost of fire insurance for a given client in a particular geographical unit. The value of a future claim of fire damage within a given period of time for a geographical area is unknown. However, the frequency and cost of damage from fires in the area, and profit associated with providing insurance to a client over a given time period, can be statistically estimated with useful accuracy from relevant fire histories, time periods, and demographic assumptions. The reliability of such actuarial estimates can be viewed as the relatively stable profitability of many insurance companies.

(3) Uncertainty associated with investing.

Consider the uncertainty of the value of investing in a new business project. Success depends on the nature of future events such as consumer taste at the time of launch of a project, existence of competing innovations, cost at time of delivery, state of the domestic and global economy, and as well as changes in regulations among many other issues. Any estimate of the probability of success depends on little more than the notion of business acumen. An investor has no other instrument than their own faculty of judgment. Knightian uncertainty of the probability of investing success is not only unknown it is fundamentally unknowable. Business decision uncertainty is a transcendent risk characterizing investment in equity and other financial markets.

Defenders of neoclassical expected utility theory, such as Savage (1954), argue that an enumeration of all states that are likely to occur in the future can be made and an evaluation of value and a probability assessment assigned that can convert the uncertainty associated with an investment risk decision into the VM rationality framework. But Knight reminds us that the necessary requirement of a reliable enumeration of all possible future states associated with a business investment view of security risk and its value is not possible. Perceptions of the future that inform current judgment will impact the future that evolves over time even as future perceptions are the basis for current judgment. Moreover, the self-referential world of financial markets and any other social ontological reality is not stationary. In social science, the evolution of reality is particularly affected by judgments made now even as they are often the result of poor forecasts of an eventual reality. Knightian financial uncertainty is of an altogether higher order than any repeatable game or reliable statistical estimation as commonly understood in an actuarial framework. It is rather the ideal context for an appropriate realistic understanding for stock market volatility and rationality. From a Knightian point of view, financial returns in an equity market are fundamentally uncertain and unreliably forecastable.

Keynes Speculative Markets

Keynes (1936) famously describes the stock market as a social group with its own dynamic of interactions, norms, and conventions. He compares success in stock market investing as a collective way of thinking analogous to being rewarded for correctly guessing who the readers of a newspaper contest would choose as the prettiest girl from a set of published photos. The key to success, he teaches, is not to pick the girl you consider the prettiest in the photos in the newspaper, but who you estimate is the one most likely chosen by the consensus of newspaper readers.

In Keynes, the newspaper contest defines a social group with rules independent of personal utility. An investor must set aside what he believes the stock is worth to estimate how the collective consciousness of the social group of investors in a market would value the stock. Winning is defined as estimating the consensus opinion within the group of stock investors.

As in Knight (1921), Keynes dismisses the notion of stock price based on objective fundamental value. Keynes' radical vision of stock market uncertainty is investor rationality in a sociological context. This is consistent with how Durkheim (1893, 1897) describes the nature of a sociological entity external to the individual. The group represents a social consciousness invested with coercive power and a distinct sense of rationality. Agents are not irrational but informed with best interest norms of behavior in the context of the collective.[2] Such a view limits the value of an assessment of the fundamental worth of a firm independent of market liquidity and elevates the importance of stock market themes, investment fashions, and the influence of sponsorship by large financial institutions as the major factors of stock price formation. Investors should be sensitive to fads and popular themes with stock investors. Stock price is a conditionally socially defined rational consensus within the group of investors investing in the market. In radical uncertainty, objective fundamental value may no longer exist. Keynes and Durkheim give us a very valuable set of considerations for a viable sociological theory of equity markets. It is of interest to note that Keynes was known to be a very successful investor.

Markowitz (1952) and Investing Norms

When Markowitz was searching for an understanding of the stock market, he asked himself a simple question: How do informed investors invest? In the process, he identifies institutional mutual fund managers as a social group that represents informed investor practice. His epiphany was to observe that fund manager behavior could be modeled as parametric quadratic programming. The Markowitz MV efficient frontier and the essential notion of portfolio optimality for modern finance are born. Consistent with Knight and Keynes, security selection and risk-return estimation are exogenous to the Markowitz procedure. A simple investigation of the behavioral norms of a social group of investors comes to define the bedrock of twentieth-century modern finance in theory and practice.

The mutual fund manager represents a financial intermediary that facilitates investor activity in the same way that a trader facilitates the execution of the trade or the bank manager enables savings for clients' future needs. The intermediation is sociological in the sense that it describes the rationality of a social group consensus as the dynamic interaction for investment purposes. The consensus of mutual fund managers representing social group norms comes to define much of modern financial theory and asset management.

From the perspective of a hundred years, we find in the work of Knight, Keynes, and Markowitz, a remarkable independent consensus of the essential nature of equity capital market risk. We now follow the thread they provide of stock market group rationality from a contemporary perspective.

---

[2] In its simplest form, norm behavior often has the benefit of time efficient.

The Prisoner's Dilemma

Neoclassical finance is based on self-interest utility maximization. From the point of view of stability as well as common sense, why would anyone not act in their own self-interest? But self-interest can be toxic and self-defeating in some cases. If so, how could the evolution of behavioral norms in financial markets not be chaotic and self-destructive?

The prisoner's dilemma is an iconic game theory framework for understanding the limitations of best interest social interaction in a rational framework. The familiar story is that two prisoners are detained by the police who are suspected of stealing a large sum of money but held for a minor infraction. The police propose to each prisoner individually to let them go free if they provide evidence that the other is guilty of stealing the money. If neither confess they both serve a light sentence. If one confesses and the other does not, the one who defects goes free and the other serves a heavy sentence.

As game theorists note, rational behavior is always to defect. But if both defects, they both get a heavy sentence. It is always possible that neither would defect, which is the best outcome for both as a two-person social group. Cooperation which means not defecting comes at a very high price if the other defects. This is a classic cooperation social dilemma. If the game is only played once, as in the prisoner game scenario, the rational decision is defect and both, as a social group, suffer from defection.

Multiperiod Character of Cooperative Social Norms

The interesting paradox of social interaction and prisoner game rationality is that much actual social behavior does not exhibit pure self-interest. Why does anyone tip a server in a restaurant when you are just passing through? Yet the majority of people do tip even in this presumably absurd rational self-interest context. How to reconcile the vast majority of quotidian behavior that is essentially cooperative and often altruistic with individual utility maximization that mandates self-interest? Why does a social group context often exhibit individual non-self-interest behavior?

One of the most important and successful examples of the evolution of cooperative social norms by rational though minimally informed agents interacting over time is a multiperiod coordination game framework as presented in Axelrod (1984). His tournaments illustrate the successes and failures of various individual social norms of behavior in a multiperiod setting of the prisoner's dilemma game. In the Axelrod game, prison sentences are redefined in terms of economic payoffs where the benefits of cooperating and defecting are the same. In the multiperiod game, agents may randomly encounter but will remember each other's prior behavior in each encounter. While Axelrod tested many kinds of defect and cooperation policies what emerged surprised many. The winning strategy on average—tit for tat—represented cooperating as much as possible but firmly defecting if the prior encounter had resulted in a defection and never deviating from defection until the most recent encounter was a cooperating decision by the opponent.

The Axelrod tournament is an example of agent-based model (ABM) simulation of best interest evolutionary norms of multiple agents and random encounters with simple rationality rules of engagement. As the game progresses, some agents practicing a tit-for-tat strategy may accumulate much wealth often dominating their opponents who do not practice the cooperating strategy. But it is important to note that the cooperative strategy is not always economically dominant and the sum total of economic wealth of the social group may be adversely affected. While a given simulation can reflect the consequence of perverse behavior randomly, more interestingly deviant or perverse strategies can often result in overall poor results on average for the social group. The cautionary tale here is that the benevolent evolution of social norms is not guaranteed when social groups have to evolve under many kinds of random exogenous events and entrants of mutants or deviants. The analogous behavior in financial markets includes fads, fashions, crashes, and geopolitical events.

Social Norm Stability

Young (2012) provides a simple example of the power of stable norms in a prototypical ABM evolutionary process associated with the development of rental contracts. Most people prefer a standard rental contract. This is because rental negotiation can focus on price and occupancy and avoid concerns of all kinds of legal issues or restrictions of enforceability that may be part of renting a property. The interesting question is: How did standard contracts become standard? Rental contracts share the same basic Keynesian and Knightian views of radical uncertainty of the evolutionary dynamics of rational but limited-information agents in a social group. A long period of experimentation and social dynamic evolution led to standard contracts. Importantly, such contracts do not need to represent optimal decisions so long as they serve the purpose of facilitating rental activity and become what everyone has come to expect. Rental contracts have evolved into a highly stable social institution or convention. Deviating from such contracts may often be risky and costly for either buyer or seller.

There are a great variety of social and economic institutions that have evolutionary patterns similar to a rental contract. Language represents a social group with interactive conventions. All forms of money, patents, courtship, codes of dress, and marriage conventions, while reflecting their own evolutionary patterns, often have similar development of stable norms and institutions. Institutions are not willed but emerge from experimentation and often historical accident, the product of the decisions of many over time, where codifications of existing practices came into being through social evolution.

Pure Coordination Games Rationality

Imitation is arguably the most fundamental of sociological processes. The laws of imitation or mimetism are to sociology what heredity is to biology, and what gravitation is to astronomy.[3] It is hardly possible to overstate the importance of the imitation drive in social interactions, financial or otherwise. Humans have a strong innate capacity and need for imitation even as little children.

Pure coordination games represent a simple yet powerful framework for a large class of cooperative ABMs for low-information rational social interaction agents. The process can show how stable norms and conventions can emerge without the need of external mediation or rationality axioms beyond multiperiod prisoner dilemma self-interest.[4] The social interaction of a universe of agents can reflect a simple even myopic and stable rationality very different from VM game theory axiomatic behavior.

Consider the evolutionary process from mimetic behavior in a simple multiperiod coordination game. In each play of the game, each individual chooses a number from 1 to 100. Each person's award will be proportional to the number of other persons in the social group who make the same choice. In the first round, the most popular number chosen by the group is likely random. On subsequent plays, individuals informed from prior results start to guess the numbers likely to attract the most votes. Over time multiple

---

[3] Ellwood (1901).

[4] In the U.S., the Security and Exchange Commission is tasked to impose regulations to make transactions fair to all participants.

social norms may evolve that characterize the interactive dynamics of the social group. Participants may often have a vested interest in sustaining a bullish bubble for as long as possible. The key is that there is no objective sense of value beyond group agreement. Fads and crashes can emerge and disappear spontaneously. Another group of players may likely lead to significantly different number norms. The possible disruptive impact of mutants and perverse agents is often easy to understand given the fragility of the conventions that arise. This possible convergence, in the purest sense of the game, is a matter of total indifference. All that is important for doing well in the game is that there is mimetic agreement among some on a favorite number or numbers.

A coordination game can be a valuable framework for understanding the evolution of equity market norms and the social group rationality of individual investor self-interest behavior. In the numbers coordination game, rational behavior is that of naive self-interest agents acting on limited information where prices and markets coordinate economic activity. It's a very human form of economic behavior and very different from the mathematical equations typical of scholarly academic presentations and research characteristic of much contemporary social science publications. Coordination agents adapt, gather information, act sensibly, and may often, though not always, iterate to dominant strategies. Agents are not devoid of rationality, but they are not hyper-rational as in VM rationality. Multiperiod evolutionary forces substitute for the implausible degree of individual rationality required by VM-Savage axioms. Such behavior is strikingly consistent with how the stock exchanges historically evolved in London, Amsterdam, and New York.

Local Market Equilibrium

There are important conditions for an ABM model in an economic incentive market to iterate to a kind of local equilibrium. Agents in the population may not be informed but need to adjust their behavior to what they learn from recent interactions with others. The actions of agents become precedents that influence others. The self-interest mimetism that arises comes from a desire of fair dealing in a transaction. Memory can be bounded or not depending on how best to model the social interaction process of price formation. The rules for behavior emerge from the interaction of myopic uninformed agents, each of whom is concerned only with maximizing his or her own welfare. Such actions operate naturally in the normal course of financial incentive interactions.

The process will likely be affected by many random perturbations from a variety of exogenous factors. In social interactions in a financial market, risk aversion is likely operative. Regulation of interactions tend to emerge that are efficient and socially fair. Market equilibrium, to the extent it may exist, is likely to have limited duration. This notion of evolutionary financial markets should be recognizable to investment professionals. Investor interactions are essentially self-referential where imitation or fair price dominates the willingness to transact.

Stock Market Evolutionary Norms[5]

What is the nature of the conventions that emerge? They may represent stability points in investor beliefs, such as value stock investing, functioning as a "favorite" number in a coordination game, and may have limited duration. They may be conventions or beliefs that nobody may believe. In this context, market price is detached from any notion of private value. This is the paradox at the heart of mimetic agent-based market efficiency. It is a very different and more realistic way of thinking about the dynamic social processes driving financial markets.

Agents in a financial market have a wide diversity of views that makes it capable of adapting to changes and avoid becoming rigid and stale. This is one of the most important benefits of a well-functioning mimetic market. Financial market ecosystems can generate a variety of perceptions of consensus value that make it capable of surviving significant changes from exogenous sources in a given time period. Adapting to changes in the financial and economic environment requires a sufficiently large variety of stable states such as convention habitats to cope with perturbations. This diversity has to be large but not too large in order not to tip the functioning of the system into chaos. There is tension between the need for variation to accommodate new information and a need for homogeneity to maintain a coherent structure and functioning. This dynamic requires an evolving system that does not exist too far from a stable norm-habitat like equilibrium to evolve and respond to the global financial environment. Self-organizing feedback structures constrain and enable future actions. Regulatory mechanisms allow the system to change and respond to the environment.

---

[5] Young (2012) provides a number of examples of sociological ABMs and their evolutionary paths and properties.

Sources for Financial Conventions

Stock market norms and investment strategy conventions often arise from sponsorship associated with the selling of financial products from large brokerage companies and investment banks. Brokers traditionally have a morning call where the sales group is told what stocks and strategies to promote on calls to clients and advisors during the day. The brute financial power of major financial institutions for forming norms and conventions can be little overstated. This process is magnified by a 24-hour business media news cycle that needs to constantly develop new stories and issues to attract listeners and readers. Asset managers themselves are important sources of norms and themes because they need to update and sell their views and strategies to clients. Consultants also require something to sell to be paid for their services. The power of academic research based on long-term historical studies has had much influence in institutional asset management. This enormous self-referential process operative virtually continuously creates the evolving norms and conventions that motivate and finance stock market activity.

While mimetism is relatively self-regulating, it is highly vulnerable to all manner of informational volatility and misinformation. In the torrent of financial information and sensitivity to global geopolitical factors, a single law of objective valuation is unlikely to exist or persist.

Negative and Positive Feedback Markets

Orléan (2014) is a contemporary economist whose views are heavily influenced by Keynes' sociological framework for financial markets and Knight's concept of economic uncertainty. His perspective of financial markets questions the importance of objective or fundamental value for security pricing. Orléan argues that liquidity in an equity market is the primary justification for price. His rationale focuses on a parsing of the characteristics of negative and positive feedback capital markets.

Negative Feedback Markets

A negative feedback market is one familiar to financial theoreticians and professionals. It is a market where the concept of supply and demand operates; the greater the supply the lower the price and vice versa. In this context, a market may often exist in a relative state of equilibrium where price essentially reflects relatively stable exogenous economic factors. For example, in a commodity market, supply is necessarily limited and prices tend to adjust over time to equilibrate demand. Absent of geopolitical influences, classical utility preference theory is likely operative. It is a framework consistent with neoclassical finance. Participants can be assumed to have fixed preferences and transactions that do not affect the stability of preferences. The function of the market is to distribute limited goods satisfying exogenous desires. It is a self-correcting process where for substitutable goods such as commodities an increase in price reduces demand.

Positive Feedback Markets

In a positive feedback market, the law of supply and demand is not necessarily operative. Demand does not necessarily decrease with increasing price, and competition is not necessarily stabilizing. Orléan distinguishes four types of positive feedback markets.

Information asymmetry.

An investor with a belief of more reliable information than the market will want to transact. As a consequence, price may change, and utility may increase, if other agents perceive and act on the belief of new reliable information.

Increasing returns to adoption.

A good may change in value for no other reason than because of an increase in the number of adopting agents. As a consequence, investor utility may increase from a desirable change in consensus price.

Price based on prestige.

A good may be associated with pure fashionableness. This is a case of exchange-based pricing and not any kind of objective change in value.

Price based on the need for liquidity.

Price is the consequence of available agents willing to trade continuously based on mimetic rational behavior. The continuing desire for liquidity by agents in a market is the underlying reason of consensus price formation and the ultimate source of investor value.

Financial fashions or fads such as internet stocks in the 1990s are an example of unstable positive feedback behavior in a capital market. In contrast, the desirability of an iPhone may be an example of stable positive feedback behavior due to increased utility simply from an increase in the number of users. Keynes' newspaper competition is also an example of stable positive feedback behavior, where the principle of value is defined within interactions in the social group and where preference is not classic individual utility function based. The commonality and essential principle is that the value of exchange is not definable in advance via fundamental value or supply and demand. Price exists only at the moment of transaction and the likely result of the existence of liquidity and the consequence of mimetic rational behavior.

Fair Exchange

Orléan's use of mimetism to characterize the social interaction of willing agents supplying liquidity in the stock market is fundamentally the notion of fair exchange. In a financial transaction, you want to be treated the same way others were treated before you. You desire to transact at or near the price obtained by the prior investor; you don't want to pay more than the previous buyer or sell for less than the prior seller. The notion of a fair price is not related to the fundamental value of a security or the fixed utility preference of an individual but of a norm of a mimetic or time efficient social interaction in a highly liquid market at the moment of exchange.

Consider the opposite scenario, an exchange without liquidity or agents unwilling to provide a trade at a fair price. Why would I want to invest in such an exchange? A widespread perception of an unfair market would surely lead to reduced economic activity. The notion of fair price is fundamental to the viability of the functioning of a market at all times all things the same.

In Orléan and Keynes, the prices in stock markets reflect the interactions of a self-referential social group geared by mimetism with agents in a state of shared ignorance. Stocks have value at a point in time because others value them and are ready to transact. Trading is not the property of the good but of willing agents in the market. Market price is a mimetic reference point, and, in a liquid market, all are speculators.

Speculation is required for the full advantage of liquidity to exist. Otherwise, prices may be stale. In a well-functioning speculative financial market dominated by fair exchange, investors can trade freely in a world where shares are instantly exchangeable for money.

Liquid Market Rationality

Keynes and Orléan diverge when they try to rationalize capital market behavior. On the one hand, Keynes attributes what an investment is worth to investors under the influence of "mass psychology."[6] Keynes' observation

---

[6] Keynes (1936, pp. 154–155).

provides a caveat emptor warning for stock market investors with no fundamental rationale for behavior. On the other hand, Orléan finds a code of
social interaction for rationalizing the promise of a fair return at withdrawal.
Given a nearly hundred-year span of knowledge since Keynes, contemporary
sociology and psychology can provide a more informed framework for stock
market rationality.

The Stock Market as a Unique Financial Intermediary

Where does the continuous demand for liquidity in financial markets come
from? We claim it is an essential characteristic of major stock markets as a
unique financial intermediary for investors. Equity markets provide liquid
time-shift intermediation for meeting investor future obligations. We explore
these issues further below.

Private Ownership Versus Security Risk

Entrepreneurial ownership of a firm represents very risky capital because it
is immobile. If the firm needs capital to survive and it is not available from
the owners or partners or a new investor, dissolution of the enterprise may
be necessary. A liquid stock market enables the conversion of immobile to
liquid capital. Firm listing on an equity exchange converts ownership of the
firm into a liquid asset with an observable value. Capital is liberated from the
infinite horizon risk of a firm. Creditors and owners can liquidate holdings
whenever they need. This transformation requires a price acceptable to all
investors. On the other hand, liquid markets can't dispose of assets. I can't
sell anything if there are no buyers. Liquidity is not a property of the asset; it
is a property of the market itself. Liquid price reflects a collective belief free
of capital immobility.

Financial Intermediation

The stock market, like a bank or fixed income investments, operates as
a financial intermediary for investors. Each enable a time-shift facility for
the value of invested funds. In the case of a commercially viable bank, the
promised benefit is likely a zero-real return value of savings at time of withdrawal. In the case of a well-managed bond fund, and ignoring default risk,
the promised benefit is generally fixed at maturity. In contrast, the value
of equity investment depends on the state of domestic and foreign capital
markets at withdrawal independent of the length of the investment period.

Motivation is liquid market time-shift expectation of a fair return on savings at an unspecified time of withdrawal. It is the intermediation framework of choice for long-term investing objectives for investor and institution alike.

While historically, major equity markets have often provided a significant positive benefit for bearing equity risk on average over sufficiently long investment horizons, any given finite time period may often be associated with losses rather than gains. A popular strategy to manage point-in-time equity risk may be to consider a well-diversified risk-targeted portfolio such as a 60/40 stock/non-stock portfolio of index funds. While such considerations are important for practice, they do not impact our objective for understanding the fundamental financial role and nature of liquid equity markets.

Investor Risk Aversion

Keynes' and Orléan's discussion of fair exchange rationality of a speculative market tends to ignore the role of investor risk aversion. Agents in a financial coordination game are likely to find stable but different risk habitats as is conventionally observed in stock markets. A spectrum of norms and conventions in modern capital markets likely evolve naturally in such a risk-habitat norm creation process. This is because "value" investing may appeal to investors with high risk aversion and a preference of avoiding volatile stocks; "growth" investing may appeal to lower risk aversion investors; "market" investing may appeal to less informed or conventional risk aversion investors. Such considerations fit naturally in a Markowitz efficient frontier as a universal framework for investment choice.

Security Relative Valuation

The ubiquitous relative value framework widely used by security analysts and strategists is a necessary artifact of a mimetic market. It is essentially the only available valuation framework that can reflect security pricing. No one knows the absolute value of a stock. It is possible, however, to define value relative to competing securities or factors such as industries, sectors, lines of business, leverage, management, and global exposure. It is exactly what the most common tools of stock valuation by security analysts—earnings-to-price, book-market-to-price, and other so-called fundamentals of a security—provide for pricing. Such activity mirrors the essence of a self-referential process and what the equity market promises to deliver to the investor at time of withdrawal.

Statistical Nature of Evolutionary Social Markets

A simple model for the return generation process of a mimetic financial market framework is a compound Poisson-Gaussian distribution. Financial markets are necessarily highly sensitive to unforecastable exogenous factors that can account for unstable regimes and price cascades. A Poisson distribution reflects a simple stochastic process of jumps in firm values where unexpected events occur randomly in time. A compound Poisson-Gaussian return distribution provides a conceptual framework for random geopolitical and market events where regimes of relative calm can be represented by a Gaussian process impacted by random events from many sources and intensities. Both the Gaussian and Poisson jump intensities can vary in time as a realistic framework for disruptions in relatively stable periods of financial market behavior.

It is interesting to consider the implications of the psychological-physical process of agents at the moment of exchange in financial markets. The process of deciding to buy or sell is often fraught with substantial emotional uncertainty. In trading parlance, it is called "pulling the trigger." Only at the moment of the actual trading decision is price revealed. In modern mathematical psychology, human decision making is probabilistic. The biological process that corresponds to the decision to trade will necessarily be reflected in electrical activity in the synapses of the brain. The emotional energy associated with the trading decision at a given time conceptually resembles the process in physics of enabling the measurement of the location of the electron at the moment of measurement in a quantum interaction.

Conclusions

The sociological rationality of fair exchange financial markets is no more and no less than the evolutionary process of best effort agents in the context of shared ignorance and the propensity of precedent following. It is a theory of financial equilibrium based on minimal agent rationality that is a social self-referential dynamical process. Price exists as an external norm at the moment of exchange with agents that adapt to a social consensus of self-interest with respect to a variety of conventions and institutions established by predecessors. It is a systematic framework where market rationality is very human, very fragile, and highly susceptible to exogenous disruptive factors of all kinds.

The emergence of mimetic price behavior in an exchange can be affected by memory and learning. In a shared ignorance context, it is no longer a surprise to encounter fads, bubbles, frenzies, and crashes. Conventions and norms may survive and may be useful for a period of time with no major Poisson events. During local equilibrium volatility regimes, investing norms may appear predictable and conventional. Earnings reports, business and investing themes, and other established consensus views may prosper based on what has made money recently. It can be a time when economics and geopolitical issues have not been disruptive and markets seem a vehicle of reliable investing for meeting long-term objectives. The process itself depends on many things that can change at a moment's notice. But even in the case where conventions have lasted for a period of time, there can be no guarantee of survival.

Summary

The great early twentieth-century pioneers of finance, economics, and sociological systems provide a valuable conceptual framework on the essential nature of investment behavior and portfolio optimality. Contemporary sociological and financial research provides a theoretical framework where institutions and norms of equity markets evolve naturally from shared ignorance interactions of limited-information rational agents in a social group. The social dynamics of fair exchange behavior patterns provides a realistic framework for understanding the economic fragility of financial markets and the emergence of fads, fashions, crashes, and unanticipatable exogenous events. A sociological theoretical context of financial markets highlights the importance of enabling the collective consciousness of financial markets with effective and informed regulatory policies to efficiently serve their function as financial intermediaries for long-term investing. A more realistic understanding of the nature of equity markets avoids misdirection and enables more likely effective active investment management policies and development of more reliable quantitative asset management technologies.

References

Axelrod, R. 1984. *The Evolution of Cooperation.* New York: Basic Books.

Durkheim, E. 1893. *De la division du travail social: étude sur l'organisation des sociétés supérieures.* Paris: Alcan. Trans: *The Division of Labor in Society.* W.D. Halls. New York: The Free Press, 1984.

Durkheim, E. 1897. *Le Suicide,* Paris: Alcan. Trans: *Suicide: A Study in Sociology.* J. A. Spaulding and G. Simpson. Glencoe, IL: The Free Press of Glencoe, 1951.

Ellwood, C. 1901. The Theory of Imitation in Social Psychology. *The American Journal of Sociology,* 6 (6): 721–741.

Keynes, J. 1936. *The General Theory of Employment, Interest, and Money, Economics.* London: Macmillan and Co.

Knight, F. 1921. *Risk, Uncertainty, and Profit.* Boston: Houghton Mifflin Company.

Lo, A. 2004. Adaptive Markets Hypothesis. *The Journal of Portfolio Management* 30 (5): 15–29.

Markowitz, H. 1952. Portfolio Selection. *Journal of Finance* 7 (1): 77–91.

Markowitz, H. 1959. *Portfolio Selection: Efficient Diversification of Investments,* 2nd ed. New York and Cambridge, MA: Wiley and Basil Blackwell.

Orléan, A. 2014. *The Empire of Value.* Cambridge: MIT Press.

Savage, L.J. 1954. *The Foundations of Statistics.* John Wiley & Sons.

Young, H.P. 2012. *Individual Strategy and Social Structure: An Evolutionary Theory of Institutions.* Princeton, NJ: Princeton University Press.

Epilogue

Value does not reside in objects.
It is produced by human beings acting in concert with one another.
Orléan, A. 2014. *The Empire of Value*, MIT Press, Cambridge

There have been many scientific wrong turns in human intellectual history that have had transcendental impact on society and wealth. The Copernican revolution replacing the earth with the sun as the center of the celestial universe had enormous philosophical and social repercussions of the knowable to this day. Darwin's theory of evolution of life on earth was in bitter conflict with religious tenets on the creation of the living world. The quantum revolution in physics has fundamentally altered our understanding of the physical sciences.

Wrong turns exist not only in physics, biology, philosophy, or mathematics but in our understanding of ourselves and how sociological rules and principles evolve and facilitate our lives. No less important is evidence on how humans form preferences and judgments and create socially recognized value. Even in the rarefied world of pure mathematical thought, what constitutes a valid proof remains deeply consequential and often controversial and may even ultimately affect everyday life.

© The Editor(s) (if applicable) and The Author(s), under exclusive
license to Springer Nature Switzerland AG 2023
R. O. Michaud, *Finance's Wrong Turns*,
https://doi.org/10.1007/978-3-031-21863-7

Preference Theory

Social science is preference theory based on evolving patterns of norms and conventions. While our text is informed with academic theory, it has largely focused on the social science issues that have emerged and are consequential from the perspective of an agent at the workbench.

Allais (1953) provided the first essential insight in understanding why human rational decision making under uncertainty is different from mid-twentieth-century social science dominant VM game theory axioms. Agents may often "switch" their operative utility function from concave risk-averse upward sloping to straight-line Pascal utility expectation in the context of extreme unlikely events with significant consequences.[1] Such a switching process represents nothing less than the motivation of human survival in extreme circumstances. Kahneman and Tversky (1979, 1992) provided further convincing evidence of human decision-making patterns inconsistent with VM. Such results limit broad application of straightforward mathematicalization of human decision-making models of uncertainty. It also puts much of the twentieth-century theoretical framework for social science and derivative technological innovation based on VM game theory axioms in significant doubt. Our sociological hypothesis of basic principles for a realistic preference theory and how agents function in financial markets suggests a significantly different and hopefully more relevant and productive framework for many financial markets and much of social science.

The dominant financial theory of the late twentieth century, the Capital Asset Pricing Model (CAPM), was responsible for three fundamental wrong turns for finance: (1) VM game theory axioms as the definition of human rational decision making under uncertainty; (2) approximation of expected utility in terms of mean-variance quadratic utility; (3) regression analysis of portfolio risk in terms of a CAPM framework. A fourth wrong turn is VM game theory that inherited the Gödel (1931) limitations of any consistent logical system large enough to include a metric.

The fifth wrong turn—Markowitz optimization—was an operations research framework inconsistent with the level of uncertainty endemic in investment information. However, the technology required to address the limitations of Markowitz optimization were two or more decades in future computer science and statistical methodological development.

---

[1] The utility function switching character of how humans think is very much consistent with Pascal's wager (1925). Allais was undoubtedly familiar with Pascal's thought, an important part of his French philosophical and cultural heritage.

Our purpose has been to describe a more realistic understanding of the nature and fragility of equity capital markets for more effective asset management practice. Financial markets are endemically unstable precisely because they are highly sensitive to all manner of exogenous forces that can disrupt consensus norms in a shared ignorance market where the laws of supply and demand are not operative.

A Sociological Context

An equity market that functions as a self-referential positive feedback system provides a valuable financial intermediary with a non-traditional perspective on economic value. Buyers and sellers in a state of shared ignorance may want to limit the impact of historical studies of geopolitical events, innovations, and fashions while implementing more effective statistical technology. Our theoretical framework does not invalidate the development of more reliable technology for building and managing investment portfolios. Improvements of the Markowitz framework for portfolio risk management and contemporary statistical methodology may be of significant value if the dynamic sociological character of equity markets is understood and fundamental limitations of back testing validation avoided.

This report has been largely concerned with the sociological nature of major equity markets and a generalization of the Markowitz MV investment theory and practice. Our proposals may also be useful in fixed income investment in certain cases. On the other hand, significant limitations may exist for many kinds of financial securities, strategies, and markets where supply and demand principles are operative. Note, however, that exchange-traded funds are equities of fixed income, property, and other financial securities that are all within the framework presented here.

For investors, the single most important risk factor is unforecastable risk. It is the reason why markets may not be information efficient but rather simply very difficult to estimate reliably. It is the main reason why effective diversification is the only reliable method for risk management over time. The global economy reflects exogenous highly unpredictable economic and market factors that make forecasts on individual securities essentially unforecastable over any significant time period. While Keynes' "mass psychology" factor does not fully reflect a twenty-first-century view of understanding of capital market volatility and contemporary sociology, the impact is much the same.

References

Allais, M. 1953. Le comportement de l'homme rationnel devant le risque: Critique des postulats et axioms de l'école Americaine. *Econometrica* 21 (4): 503–546.

Allais, M. 1988. The General Theory of Random Choices in Relation to the Invariant Cardinal Utility Function and the Specific Probability Function. In *Risk, Decision and Rationality*, ed. B. Munier, 233–289. Dordrecht: Reidel.

Axelrod, R. 1984. *The Evolution of Cooperation*. New York: Basic Books.

Archie, L.C 2006. Blaise Pascal, 'Pascal's Wager'. *Philosophy of Religion* (June 26).

Bachelier, L. 1900. *Theorie de la speculation*. Gauthiers-Villars.

Beale, E.M.L. 1955. On Minimizing a Convex Function Subject to Linear Inequalities. *Journal of the Royal Statistical Society (B)* 17: 173–184.

Beale, E.M.L. 1959. On Quadratic Programming. *Naval Research Logistics Quarterly* 6 (3): 227–243.

Black, F., and R. Litterman. 1992. Global Portfolio Optimization. *Financial Analysts Journal* 48 (5): 28–43.

Blin, J. and S. Bender. 1994. Arbitrage and the Structure of Risk: A Mathematical Analysis. Working Paper, APT, Inc.

Blin, J., S. Bender, and J.B. Guerard, Jr. 1997. Earnings Forecasts, Revisions and Momentum in the Estimation of Efficient Market-Neutral Japanese and U.S. Portfolios. In *Research in Finance*, ed. A. Chen, 15. Greenwich, CT: JAI Press.

Bourbaki, 1948. L'Architecture des Mathématicques. In *Les Grand Courants de la Pensée Mathématicques*, ed. F. Le Lionnais, 33–47. Paris.

Bourbaki, N. 1949. Foundations of Mathematics for the Working Mathematician. *Journal of Symbolic Logic* 14: 1–8.

Brinson, G., L.R. Hood and G. Beebower. 1986. Determinants of Portfolio Performance. *Financial Analyst Journal* 42 (4).

© The Editor(s) (if applicable) and The Author(s), under exclusive license to Springer Nature Switzerland AG 2023
R. O. Michaud, *Finance's Wrong Turns*,
https://doi.org/10.1007/978-3-031-21863-7

Campbell, J., A. Lo, and A.C. Mackinlay. 1997. *The Econometrics of Financial Markets.* Princeton University Press.

Cauchy, A. 1821. Cours D'Analyse de L'Ecole Royales Polytechnique. Librarie du Roi et de la Bibliotheque du Roi, Paris.

Clarke, R., H. deSilva, and S. Thorley. 2002. Portfolio Constraints and the Fundamental Law of Active Management. *Financial Analysts Journal* 58 (5): 48–66.

Clarke, R., H. deSilva, and S. Thorley. 2006. The Fundamental Law of Active Portfolio Management. *Journal of Investment Management* 4 (3): 54–72.

Choquet, G. 1953–1954. Theory of Capacities. *Annales Institut Fourier* 5: 131–295.

Church, A. 1936. An Unsolvable Problem of Elementary Number Theory. *American Journal of Mathematics* 58 (2): 345–363.

Dixit, A. 2012. Paul Samuelson's Legacy. *Annual Reviews of Economics* 4: 1–31.

Durkheim, E. 1893. *De la division du travail social: étude sur l'organisation des sociétés supérieures.* Paris: Alcan. Trans: *The Division of Labor in Society.* W.D. Halls. New York: The Free Press, 1984.

Durkheim, E. 1895. *Les Règles de la méthode sociologique.* Paris: Alcan. Trans: *The Rules of Sociological Method and Selected Texts on Sociology and Its Method.* W. D. Halls, S. Lukes, ed. New York: The Free Press, 1982.

Durkheim, E. 1897. *Le Suicide,* Paris: Alcan. Trans: *Suicide: A Study in Sociology.* J.A. Spaulding and G. Simpson. Glencoe, IL: The Free Press of Glencoe, 1951.

Ellwood, C. 1901. The Theory of Imitation in Social Psychology. *The American Journal of Sociology* 6 (6): 721–741.

Fama, E. 1970. Efficient Capital Markets: A Review of Theory and Empirical Work. *Journal of Finance* 25: 383–417.

Fama, E.F., and K.R. French. 1992. The Cross-Section of Expected Stock Returns. *Journal of Finance* 47 (2): 427–446.

Fama, E.F., and K.R. French. 2014. A Five-Factor Asset Pricing Model. *Journal of Financial Economics* 116: 1–22.

Farmer, J., and A. Lo. 1999. Frontiers of Finance: Evolution and Efficient Markets. *Proceedings of the National Academy of Sciences of the United States of America* 96 (18): 9991–9992.

Fennema, H., and T. Bezembinder. 1995. Book Review: J. Quiggin, 'Generalized Expected Utility: The Rank Dependent Model.' *Acta Psychologica* 88: 79–81.

Frahm, G. 2015. A Theoretical Foundation of Portfolio Resampling. *Theory and Decision* 79 (1): 107–132.

Frege, G. 1893/1903. Grundgesetze der Arithmetik, begriffsschriftlich abgeleitet (2 volumes: Jena, 1893, 1903).

Frost, P., and J. Savarino. 1988. For Better Performance: Constrain Portfolio Weights. *Journal of Portfolio Management* 15 (1): 29–34.

Graham, B., and D. Dodd. 1934. *Security Analysis: Principles and Techniques.* New York: McGraw-Hill.

Gödel, K. 1931. Uber formal unentscheid Satze der Principia Mathematica und verwandter Systeme, I. Trans: On Formally Undecidable Propositions of Principia

Mathematica and Related Systems I. Monash. Mathematical Physics 38: 173–198.

Grinold, R. 1989. The Fundamental Law of Active Management. *Journal of Portfolio Management* 15 (3): 30–37.

Grinold, R., and R. Kahn. 1995. *Active Portfolio Management: Quantitative Theory and Applications*. Chicago: Probus Publishing Company.

Grinold, R., and R. Kahn. 1999. *Active Portfolio Management*, 2nd ed. New York: McGraw-Hill.

Grossman, S., and J. Stiglitz. 1986. On the Impossibility of Informationally Efficient Markets. *American Economic Review* 70 (3): 393–408.

Hensel, C., D. Ezra and J. Ilkiw 1991. The Importance of the Asset Allocation Decision. *Financial Analyst Journal* (July–August 1991).

Hilbert, D. 1980 (1899). *Grundlagen de Geometrie*. 2nd ed. Chicago: Open Court.

Hilbert, D.P. Bernays. *Grundlagen der Mathematik* (2 volumes; Berlin 1934 and 1938).

Hume, D. 1748. *An Enquiry Concerning Human Understanding*. London: Oxford.

Hume, D. 1784. *Philosophical Essays Concerning Human Understanding*. London.

Jobson, D., and B. Korkie. 1981. Putting Markowitz Theory to Work. *Journal of Portfolio Management* 7 (4): 70–74.

Kahneman, D., and A. Tversky. 1979. Prospect Theory: An Analysis of Decision Under Risk. *Econometrica* 47 (2): 263–291.

Kendall, M.G., and R.M. Sundrum. 1953. Distribution-Free Methods and Order Properties. *Review of the International Statistical Institute* 3: 124–134.

Keynes, J. 1936. *The General Theory of Employment, Interest, and Money, Economics*. London: Macmillan and Co.

Knight, F. 1921. *Risk, Uncertainty, and Profit*. Boston: Houghton Mifflin Company.

Kritzman, M. 2006. Are Optimizers Error Maximizers? *Journal of Portfolio Management* 32 (4): 66–69.

Kroll, Y., H. Levy, and H. Markowitz. 1984. Mean-Variance Versus Direct Utility Maximization. *Journal of Finance* 39 (1): 47–61.

Leibniz, G.W. 1875–1890. Die Philosophischen Schriften von Gottfried Wilhelm Leibniz (G), 7 Vols, ed. C.I. Gerhardt (Berlin: Weidman). Translated by Robert Ariew and Daniel Garber, Philosophical Essays (Indianapolis: Hackett Publishing Company, 1989).

Levy, H., and H. Markowitz. 1979. Approximating Expected Utility by a Function of the Mean and the Variance. *American Economic Review* 69 (3): 308–317.

Lintner, John. The Valuation of Risk Assets and the Selection of Risky Investments in Stock Portfolios and Capital Budgets. *Review of Economics and Statistics* (February 1965).

Lo, A. 2004. Adaptive Markets Hypothesis. *The Journal of Portfolio Management* 30 (5): 15–29.

Lohr, S. 1988. A French Economist Wins Nobel. *New York Times*.

Markowitz, H. 1952a. Portfolio Selection. *Journal of Finance* 7 (1): 77–91.

Markowitz, H. 1952b. Utility of Wealth. *Journal of Political Economy* 60 (2).

Markowitz, H. 1955. The Optimization of a Quadratic Function Subject to Linear Constraints. *Naval Research Logistics Quarterly* 3: 111–133.

Markowitz, H. 1956. The Optimization of a Quadratic Function Subject to Linear Constraints. *Naval Research Logistics Quarterly* 3 (1/2): 111–133.

Markowitz, H. 1959. *Portfolio Selection: Efficient Diversification of Investments*, 2nd ed. New York and Cambridge MA: Wiley and Basil Blackwell.

Markowitz, H. 1987. *Mean-Variance Analysis in Portfolio Choice and Capital Markets*. New Hope, Pennsylvania: Fabozzi Associates.

Markowitz, H. 2005. Market Efficiency: A Theoretical Distinction and So What? *Financial Analysts Journal* 61 (5): 17–30.

Markowitz, H., and N. Usmen. 2003. Resampled Frontiers Versus Diffuse Bayes: An Experiment. *Journal of Investment Management* 1 (4): 9–25.

Markowitz, H., and G.G. Todd. 2000. *Mean-Variance Analysis in Portfolio Choice and Capital Markets*. New Jersey: John Wiley & Sons.

Mehta, J., C. Starmer and R. Sugden 1994. The Nature of Salience: An Experimental Investigation of Pure Coordination Games. *American Economic Review* 84 (3): 658–673.

Menger, C. 1892. On the Origin of Money. Caroline Foley (trans.). *Economic Journal* 2: 239–255.

Menger, C. 1892/2005. La monnaie, mesure de valeur. *Reveu d'economie politique* 6 (1892): 159–175. Translated in Gilles Campagnolo, Carl Menger's. Money as Measure of Value. *History of Political Economy* 37 (2): 245–261.

Merton, R.C. 1987. *Journal of Finance* 42 (3): 483–510.

Michaud, R. 1985. A Scenario-Dependent Dividend Discount Model: Bridging the Gap Betbetween Top-down Investment Information and Bottom-up Forecasts. *Financial Analysts Journal* 41 (6): 49–59.

Michaud, R. 1989. The Markowitz Optimization Enigma: Is Optimized Optimal? *Financial Analysts Journal* (January–February).

Michaud, R. 1990. Demystifying Multiple Valuation Models. *Financial Analysts Journal* 46 (1): 6–8.

Michaud, R. 1993. Are Long-Short Equity Strategies Superior? *Financial Analyst Journal* 49 (6): 44–49.

Michaud, R. 1998. *Efficient Asset Management: A Practical Guide to Stock Portfolio Optimization and Asset Allocation*. Boston: Harvard Business School Press.

Michaud, R. 1999. *Investment Styles, Market Anomalies, and Global Stock Selection*. Charlottesville: Research Foundation of the Chartered Financial Institute.

Michaud, R. 2006. forthcoming. Comment on: Kritzman, M. 2006. Are Optimizers Error Maximizers? *Journal of Portfolio Management*.

Michaud, R. 2011. Dr. Harry M. Markowitz Interview with Dr. Richard O. Michaud. JOIM Conference Series San Diego, March 6. *Journal of Investment Management* 9 (4): 1–9. Available at SSRN: https://ssrn.com/abstract=2402240 or https://doi.org/10.2139/ssrn.2402240

Michaud, R. 2022. *Research Announcement: Michaud Optimization Is Expected utility Consistent and Distribution-Free Optimal*. New Frontier Institute (January).

Michaud, R., and P. Davis 1982. Valuation Model Bias and the Scale Structure of Dividend Discount Returns. *Journal of Finance* (March).

Michaud, R., D. Esch, and R. Michaud. 2012. Portfolio Monitoring in Theory and Practice. *Journal of Investment Management* 10 (4): 5–18.

Michaud, R., D. Esch, and R. Michaud. 2013. Deconstructing Black-Litterman: How to Get the Portfolio You Already Knew You Wanted. *Journal of Investment Management* 11 (1): 6–20.

Michaud, Richard O., David N. Esch, and Robert O. Michaud. 2020. Estimation Error and the Fundamental Law of Active Management: Is Quant Fundamentally Flawed? *The Journal of Investing* 29 (4): 20–30.

Michaud, R., and D. Esch. 2017. When Michaud Optimization Fails. Available at: https://newfrontieradvisors.com/media/1488/mofjan2018.pdf

Michaud, R., D. Esch, and R. Michaud. forthcoming. Comment on: Allen, D., C. Lizieri, S. Satchell 2019. 'In Defense of Portfolio Optimization: What If We Can Forecast?' *Financial Analysts Journal*.

Michaud, R., and R. Michaud 2002. Resampled Portfolio Rebalancing and Monitoring. *New Frontier Advisors Newsletter* (4th quarter).

Michaud, R., and R. Michaud. 2005. Scherer's Errors. New Frontier Newsletter.

Michaud, R., and R. Michaud. 2008a. *Efficient Asset Management: A Practical Guide to Stock Portfolio Optimization and Asset Allocation*. New York: Oxford University Press. 1st ed. 1998, originally published by Harvard Business School Press, Boston.

Michaud, R., and R. Michaud. 2008b. Estimation Error and Portfolio Optimization: A Resampling Solution. *Journal of Investment Management* 6 (1): 8–28.

Mossin, J. 1966. Equilibrium in a Capital Asset Market. *Econometrica* 34 (4): 768–783.

Newton, I. 1687. *Philosophiae Naturalis Principia Mathematica*. London: Royal Society.

Orléan, A. 2014. *The Empire of Value*. Cambridge: MIT Press.

Pascal, B. 1935. *Pensées et Opuscule Philosophique*. Paris: Librarie Hachette.

Peano, G. 1889. *Arithmetices principia, nova methodo exposita*. Torino: Bocca.

Pearson, K. 1901. On Lines and Planes of Closest Fit to Systems of Points in Space. *Philosophical Magazine* 2 (11): 559–572.

Quiggin, J. 1982. A Theory of Anticipated Utility. *Journal of Economic Behavior and Organization* 3 (4): 323–343.

Quiggin, J. 1993. *Generalized Expected Utility Theory: The Rank-Dependent Model*. London: Kluwer Academic Publishers.

Roberts, H. 1959. Stock-Market "Patterns" and Financial Analysis: Methodological Suggestions. *Journal of Finance* 14 (1): 1–10.

Roll, R. 1992. A Mean/Variance Analysis of Tracking Error. *Journal of Portfolio Management* (Summer).

Roll, R., and Stephen Ross. 1994. On the Cross-Sectional Relation Between Expected Returns and Betas. *Journal of Finance* (March).

Rosenberg, B. 1974. Extra-Market Components of Covariance in Security Returns. *Journal of Financial and Quantitative Analysis* (March).

Rosenberg, B., and W. McKibben. 1973. The Prediction of Systematic and Specific Risk in Common Stocks. *Journal of Financial and Quantitative Analysis* 8 (3): 1973.

Rosenberg, B., and J. Guy. 1973. Beta and Investment Fundamentals. *Financial Analysts Journal* 32 (3): 60–72.

Rosenberg, B., and J. Guy. 1976a. Prediction of Beta from Investment Fundamentals: Part One. *Financial Analyst Journal* 32 (3): 60–72.

Rosenberg, B., and J. Guy. 1976b. *Prediction of Beta from Investment Fundamentals: Part Two* 32 (4): 62–70.

Ross, S. 1976. The Arbitrage Theory of Capital Asset Pricing. *Journal of Economic Theory* (December).

Russell, B.D. 1903. Letter to Frege. In *Principles of Mathematics*. Cambridge.

Rummel, R.J. 1970. *Applied Factor Analysis*. Evanston: Northwestern University Press.

Samuelson, P. 1948/1980. *Economics*, 11th ed. New York: McGraw-Hill.

Samuelson, P. 1965. Proof That Properly Anticipated Prices Fluctuate Randomly. *Industrial Management Review* 6 (2).

Savage, L.J. 1954. *Foundations of Statistics*. NY: Wiley.

Scheffé, H. 1943. Statistical Inference in the Non-parametric Case. *The Annals of Mathematical Statistics* 14: 305–332.

Scherer, B. 2002. Portfolio Resampling: Review and Critique. *Financial Analysts Journal* 58 (6): 98–109.

Sharpe, W. 1963. A Simplified Model for Portfolio Analysis. *Management Science*.

Sharpe, W. 1964. Capital Asset Prices: A Theory of Market Equilibrium Under Conditions of Risk. *Journal of Finance* (September).

Sharpe, W., and L. Tint. 1990. Liabilities—A New Approach. *The Journal of Portfolio Management Winter* 16 (2): 5–10.

Schulmerich, M., Y. Leporcher, and C. Eu. 2015. *Applied Asset and Risk Management*. Heidelberg: Springer.

Schmeidler, David. 1989. Subjective Probability and Expected Utility Without Additivity. *Econometrica* 57: 571–587.

Theil, H. 1971. *Principles of Econometrics*. New York: Wiley.

Theil, H., and A.S. Goldberger. 1961. On Pure and Mixed Statistical Estimation in Economics. *International Economic Review* 2: 65–78.

Treynor, J. 1963. Implications for the Theory of Finance. Unpublished manuscript.

Turing, A. 1936. On Computable Numbers, with an Applications to the Entscheidungsproblem. *Proceedings of the London Mathematical Society* 42 (1): 230–265.

Tversky, A., and D. Kahneman. 1992. Advances in Prospect Theory: Cumulative representation of Uncertainty. *Journal of Risk and Uncertainty* 5: 297–323.

Von Neumann, J., and O. Morgenstern. 1944. *Theory of Games and Economic Behavior*. Princeton University Press.

Wakker, P. 1990. Under stochastic dominance Choquet - expected utility and anticipated utility are identical. *Theory and Decision* 29: 119–132.

Wakker, P. 1991. Under Stochastic Dominance Choquet Expected Utility and Anticipated Utility Are Identical. *Theory and Decision* 29: 119–132.

Walras, L. 1874–1877/1954. Elements of Pure Economics, or the Theory of Social Wealth. Trans. William Jaffe from 4th ed., rev. and August ed. (1926). Homewood IL. Irwin 1954.

Weiner, N. 1964. Intellectual Honesty and the Contemporary Scientist. *Technology Review* 1718 (April): 45–47.

Whitehead, A.N., and B. Russell. 1910 (1912–1913). *Principia Mathematica*, Vols. 1,2,3. Cambridge: Cambridge University Press.

Wigglesworth, R. 2021. *Trillions.* Penguin Group.

Williams, J.B. 1938. *Theory of Investment Value.* Cambridge, MA: Harvard University Press.

Wilks, S.S. 1947. Order Statistics. Address Delivered Before the Summer Meeting of the Society in New Haven by invitation of the Committee to Select Hour Speakers for Annual and Summer Meetings.

Wolfe, P. 1959. The Simplex Algorithm for Quadratic Programming. *Econometrica* 27 (3): 382–398.

Yaari, M. 1987. The Dual Theory of Choice Under Risk. *Econometrica* 55 (1): 95–115.

Young, H.P. 2012. *Individual Strategy and Social Structure: An Evolutionary Theory of Institutions.* Princeton, NJ: Princeton University Press.

Index

© The Editor(s) (if applicable) and The Author(s), under exclusive
license to Springer Nature Switzerland AG 2023
R. O. Michaud, *Finance's Wrong Turns*,
https://doi.org/10.1007/978-3-031-21863-7

CPSIA information can be obtained
at www.ICGtesting.com
Printed in the USA
LVHW052326100323
741356LV00005B/577

9 783031 218620